W9-BDZ-989

Architecture and Utopia
Design and Capitalist Development

for Giusi

Architecture and Utopia
Design and Capitalist Development

Manfredo Tafuri

Translated from the Italian by
Barbara Luigia La Penta

The MIT Press
Cambridge, Massachusetts, and London, England

Sixth printing, 1988

This is a translation of *Progetto e Utopia*, published in 1973 by Guis.
Laterza & Figli, Bari, Italy, in 1973.

Printed and bound in the United States
of America by Halliday Lithograph

Library of Congress Cataloging in Publication Data

Tafuri, Manfredo.
        Architecture and utopia.

        Translation of Progetto e utopia.
        Includes bibliographical references.
        1. Architecture and society. 2. Cities and towns — Planning.
3. Form (Aesthetics) I. Title.
NA2543.S6T3313   720   75-33128
ISBN 0-262-20033-3 (hard)
ISBN 0-262-70020-4 (paper)

Contents

Preface

This volume is the result of a reworking and sizeable enlargment of my essay, "Per una critica dell'ideologia architettonica," published in the periodical *Contropiano* (1969, no. 1).

Immediately after the publication of that essay many more or less violent stands were taken in regard to its theses. To these I have always avoided responding directly, not so much out of a lack of respect for my critics, as for reasons which must now of necessity be clarified once and for all. The essay published in *Contropiano*—in a deliberately summary and sketchy form—carried to their extreme consequences those hypotheses already expressed in my *Teorie e storia dell'architettura*. Rereading the history of modern architecture in the light of methods offered by an ideological criticism, understood in the strictest Marxist acceptance of the term, could, six years ago, furnish only a frame of reference for further examination, and only a partial and circumstantial analysis of individual problems. The journal that published this essay (and others by myself and by colleagues working along the same lines) was so clearly defined in its political history and particular line of thought and interests, that one would have supposed that many equivocal interpretations might *a priori* have been avoided.

This was not the case. By isolating the architectural problems treated from the theoretical context of the journal, the way was found to consider my essay an apocalyptic prophecy, "the expression of renunciation," the ultimate pronouncement of the "death of architecture."

And yet, what in 1968–1969 was only a working hypothesis became—especially with the research carried on at the Historical Institute of the Institute of Architecture of the University of Venice—something specific, enriched, and defined in many of its basic principles. The relationship between the historical avant-garde movements and the metropolis, the relationships between intellectual work and capitalist development, researches on German sociology of the early twentieth century, on ideology and the planning practices of the Soviet Union, on the social-democratic administration of the city, on architecture and American cities, and on the building cycle, have been the object of a collaborative program of study, and one very far indeed from pretending to have arrived at any firm and dogmatic conclusions.

Publishing now in 1975 the English edition of the book* based on my essay of 1969, I more than anyone realize the ground since covered, the changes of judgment made necessary by more accurate investigation, and the weaknesses of those first hypotheses. It seems to me, however, that on the whole those hypotheses have stood up, and that the argument can now be

---

* The original edition of this book, entitled *Progetto e Utopia*, was published in January 1973 by Laterza, Bari.

developed on the basis of analysis and documentation, and not merely on the basis of principles.

In order to discuss these principles, however, it is necessary to enter into the field of political theory as this has been developed by the most advanced studies of Marxist thought from 1960 to the present. Ideological criticism cannot be separated from this context. It is an integral part of it, and all the more so when it is conscious of its own limits and its own sphere of action.

It should be stated immediately that the critical analysis of the basic principles of contemporary architectural ideology does not pretend to have any "revolutionary" aim. What is of interest here is the precise identification of those tasks which capitalist development has taken away from architecture. That is to say, what it has taken away in general from ideological prefiguration. With this, one is led almost automatically to the discovery of what may well be the "drama" of architecture today: that is, to see architecture obliged to return to *pure architecture*, to form without utopia; in the best cases, to sublime uselessness. To the deceptive attempts to give architecture an ideological dress, I shall always prefer the sincerity of those who have the courage to speak of that silent and outdated "purity"; even if this, too, still harbors an ideological inspiration, pathetic in its anachronism.

Paradoxically, the new tasks given to architecture are something besides or beyond architecture. In recognizing this situation, which I mean to corroborate historically, I am expressing no regret, but neither am I making an apocalyptic prophecy. No regret, because when the role of a discipline ceases to exist, to try to stop the course of things is only regressive utopia, and of the worst kind. No prophecy, because the process is actually taking place daily before our eyes. And for those wishing striking proof, it is enough to observe the percentage of architectural graduates really exercising that profession.

Also, there is the fact that this decline within the profession proper has not yet resulted in a corresponding institutionally defined role for the technicians charged with building activity. For this reason one is left to navigate in empty space, in which anything can happen but nothing is decisive.

This does not mean that a lucid awareness of the present situation is not necessary. But the objective of finding this institutionally defined role cannot be achieved by presenting illusory hopes. And note that it is an objective which is still ambiguous in itself. Doing away with outdated myths, one certainly does not see on the architectural horizon any ray of an alternative, of a technology "of the working class."

Ideology is useless to capitalist development, just as it is damaging from the working-class point of view. After the studies of Fortini in *Verifica dei poteri*, and those of Tronti, Asor Rosa, and Cacciari, I feel it superfluous to turn again to *German Ideology* to demonstrate this fact. Of course, once the work of ideological criticism has been completed, there remains the problem of deciding what instruments of knowledge might be immediately useful to the political struggle. It is precisely here that my discourse must end, but certainly not by choice.

From the criticism of ideology it is necessary to pass on to the analysis of the techniques of programing and of the ways in which these techniques actually affect the vital relationships of production. That is to say, we must proceed to analyses that, in the field of building activities, are only today being attempted with the necessary precision and coherence. For those anxiously seeking an operative criticism, I can only respond with an invitation to transform themselves into analysts of some precisely defined economic sector, each with an eye fixed on bringing together capitalist development and the processes of reorganization and consolidation of the working class.

In respect to such tasks this book is only a prologue. And given the summary way in which the problems are deliberately treated, it is but a historical outline that has been worked over and verified in only some of its parts. It will be necessary to go beyond this, but in the meantime I feel it not wholly useless to present this framework of a hypothesis, which if nothing else offers its own formal completeness. And it would already be a result, if such a hypothesis were to contribute to rendering agreements and disagreements more conscious and radical.

1 Reason's Adventures: Naturalism and the City in the Century of the Enlightenment

To ward off anguish by understanding and absorbing its causes would seem to be one of the principal ethical exigencies of bourgeois art. It matters little if the conflicts, contradictions, and lacerations that generate this anguish are temporarily reconciled by means of a complex mechanism, or if, through contemplative sublimation, catharsis is achieved.

The whole phenomenology of bourgeois anguish lies in the "free" contemplation of destiny. It is impossible not to be confronted continually with the perspectives opened up by that freedom. In this tragic confrontation it is impossible not to perpetuate the experience of shock. The shock derived from the experience of the metropolis, which I shall try to analyze in this book, is in itself a way of rendering anguish "active." Munch's *Scream* already expressed the necessity of a *bridge* between the absolute "emptiness" of the individual, capable of expressing himself only by a contracted phoneme, and the passivity of collective behavior.

It is not just by chance that the metropolis, the place of absolute alienation, is at the very center of concern of the avant-garde.

From the time the capitalist system first needed to represent its own anguish—in order to continue to function, reassuring itself with that "virile objectivity" discussed by Max Weber—ideology was able to bridge the gap between the exigencies of the bourgeois ethic and the universe of Necessity.

In this book I will also try to outline the stages by which compensation in the heavens of ideology ceased to be of use.

The bourgeois intellectual's obligation to exist can be seen in the imperativeness his function assumes as a "social" mission. Among the members of the intellectual "avant-garde" there exists a sort of tacit understanding concerning their position, and the mere attempt to expose it arouses a chorus of indignant protests. Indeed, culture has identified its own function as mediator in such ideological terms that—all individual good faith aside—its cunning has reached the point where it imposes the forms of disputation and protest upon its own products. The higher the sublimation of the conflicts on a formal plane, the more hidden the cultural and social structures actually expressed by that sublimation.

Attacking the subject of architectural ideology from this point of view means trying to explain why the apparently most functional proposals for the reorganization of this sector of capitalist development have had to suffer the most humiliating frustrations—why they can be presented even today as purely objective proposals devoid of any class connotation, or as mere "alternatives," or even as points of direct clash between intellectuals and capital.

It should be stated immediately that I do not believe it to be by mere chance that many of the new and recent ideas on architecture have been gleaned from an accurate reexamination of the origins of the historical avant-garde movements. Going back to these origins, situated precisely in that period when bourgeois ideology and intellectual anticipation were intimately connected, the entire cycle of modern architecture can be viewed as a unitary development. This makes it possible to consider globally the formation of architectural ideologies and, in particular, their implications for the city.

But it will be necessary to recognize also the unitary character of the cycle undergone by bourgeois culture. In other words, it will be necessary to continually bear in mind the entire picture of its development.

It is significant that systematic research on Enlightenment architecture has been able to identify, on a purely ideological level, a great many of the contradictions that in diverse forms accompany the course of contemporary art.

The formation of the architect as an ideologist of society; the individualization of the areas of intervention proper to city planning; the persuasive role of form in regard to the public and the self-critical role of form in regard to its own problems and development; the interrelationship and opposition—at the level of formal research—between architectural "object" and urban organization: these are the constantly recurrent themes of the "Enlightenment dialectic" on architecture.

When in 1753 Laugier enunciated his theories of urban design, officially initiating Enlightenment architectural theory, his words revealed a twofold inspiration. On the one hand, that of reducing the city itself to a natural phenomenon. On the other, that of going beyond any *a priori* idea of urban organization by applying to the city the formal dimensions of the aesthetic of the picturesque. Laugier declared:

Whoever knows how to design a park well will have no difficulty in tracing the plan for the building of a city according to its given area and situation. There must be squares, crossroads, and streets. There must be regularity and fantasy, relationships and oppositions, and casual, unexpected elements that vary the scene; great order in the details, confusion, uproar, and tumult in the whole.[1]

Laugier's words are a penetrating summary of the formal reality of the eighteenth-century city. No longer archetypal schemes of order, but instead the acceptance of the antiperspective character of the urban space. And even his reference to the park has new significance: in its variety, the nature that is now called upon to form part of the urban structure does away with that comforting rhetorical and didactic naturalism that had dominated the episodic continuity of Baroque layouts from the seventeenth to the mid-eighteenth century.

Thus Laugier's call to naturalism is an appeal to the

1 M. A. Laugier, *Observations sur l'Architecture*, The Hague 1765, pp. 312–313. Note, however, that the text cited takes up ideas Laugier had advanced earlier in his *Essai sur l'Architecture*, Paris 1753 (pp. 258–265). On Laugier, see W. Herrmann, *Laugier and Eighteenth Century French Theory*, Zwemmer, London 1962. The comparison between Laugier's urban-planning theories and the projects of Gwynn and George Dance, Jr., for London is very interesting. On this see: J. Gwynn, *London and Westminster Improved*, with the *Discourse on Publick Magnificence*, London 1766; M Hugo-Brunt, "George Dance the Younger as Town-Planner (1768–1814)," *Journal of the Society of Architectural Historians*, XIV, 1955, no. 4 (with many inaccuracies); and D. Stroud, *George Dance Architect, 1714–1825*, Faber & Faber, London 1971. The best contribution to the subject is the volume by G. Teyssot, *Città e utopia nell'illuminismo inglese: George Dance il giovane*, Officina Edizioni, Rome 1974.

original purity of the act of designing the environment, and at the same time it shows an understanding of the preeminently *antiorganic* quality of the city. But there is still more. The reducing of the city to a natural phenomenon is a response to the aesthetic of the picturesque, which English empiricism had introduced as early as the first decades of the eighteenth century, and which in 1759 was given an extremely elaborate and coherent theoretical foundation by the English painter, Alexander Cozens.

To what extent Laugier's ideas on the city could have influenced Cozens' theory of landscape painting, or Robert Castell's considerations in *The Villas of the Ancients*, is not known. What is certain is that the urban invention of the French abbé and the theories of the English painter have in common a basic method, in which the tool for a critical intervention in "natural" reality is selection.[2]

We see that for the eighteenth-century theorists there was no question that the city falls within the same formal area as painting. Selectivity and criticism therefore signified the introduction into urban planning of a

2 A. Cozens, *A New Method of Assisting the Invention Drawing Original Compositions of Landscape*, London 1786. Note the significance assumed by Pope's words cited at the beginning of Cozens' treatise: "Those rules wich are discovered, not devised/ are Nature still, but Nature methodized:/ Nature, like Monarchy, is but restrained/ by the same Laws wich first herself ordained". (See G. C. Argan, *La pittura dell'Illuminismo in Inghilterra da Reynolds a Constable*, Bulzoni, Rome 1965, p. 153 ff.) The civil value attributed to Nature — subject and object of ethical-pedagogical action — here becomes the substitute for the traditional principles of authority that rationalism and sensualism were destroying. See also R. Castell, *The Villas of the Ancients*, London 1728, dedicated to Lord Burlington. On the significance of the treatises of Castell and Chambers (W. Chambers, *Designs of Chinese Buildings*, London 1757) see the fundamental essay by R. Wittkower, "English Neo-Palladianism, the Landscape Garden, China, and the Enlightenment," *L'Arte*, 1969, no. 6, pp. 18–35.

fragmentation that places on the same level, not only Nature and Reason, but also natural fragment and urban fragment.

The city, inasmuch as it is a work of man, tends to a natural condition. Thus, like the landscape painted by the artist, through critical selection the city, too, must be given the stamp of a social morality.

And it is significant that, while Laugier, like the English Enlightenment theorists, had an acute grasp of the artificial character of the urban language, neither Ledoux nor Boullée, in their works much greater innovators, ever really gave up a mythical and abstract idea of nature. Boullée's controversy with Perrault's acute anticipations of the artificiality of the architectural language is highly indicative in this regard.[3]

It is possible, but not certain, that Laugier's *city like a forest* had no other model than the varied sequence of spaces that appear on the plan of Paris drawn up by Patte, who brought together in a whole the projects for the new royal square. It is, however, certain that these conceptions were referred to by George Dance, Jr., in his project for London, a project that for eighteenth-century Europe was surely very advanced.[4] I shall therefore limit myself to registering the theoretical intuitions contained in Laugier's words, which one can see as all the more pertinent when one recalls that Le

3 On the significance of Perrault's theories (set forth principally in C. Perrault, *Les dix Livres d'Architecture de Vitruve etc.*, Paris 1673), see M. Tafuri, *"Architectura Artificialis:* Claude Perrault, Sir Christopher Wren e il dibattito sul linguaggio architettonico," *Atti del Congresso Internazionale sul Barocco,* Lecce 1971, pp. 375–398. On the controversy with Boullée, see H. Rosenau, *Boullée's Treatise on Architecture,* London 1963 (comments and notes).
4 On the activity of Dance, Jr., as city planner see the bibliography cited in note 1.

Corbusier was to rely on them in delineating the theoretical principles of his *ville radieuse*.[5]

What, on the ideological plane, does *reducing the city to a natural phenomenon* signify?

On the one hand, such an enterprise involves a sublimation of physiocratic theories: the city is no longer seen as a structure that, by means of its own accumulatory mechanisms, determines and transforms the processes of the exploitation of the soil and agricultural production. Inasmuch as the reduction is a "natural" process, ahistorical because universal, the city is freed of any considerations of a structural nature. At first, formal naturalism was used to make convincing the objective necessity of the processes put in motion by the pre-Revolutionary bourgeoisie. A bit later, it was used to consolidate and protect these achievements from any further transformation.

On the other hand, this naturalism has a function of its own, which is that of assuring to artistic activity an ideological role in the strictest sense of the term. And here it is significant that, in exactly the moment when bourgeois economy began to discover and invent its own categories of action and judgment, giving to "values" contents directly commeasurable with the dictates of new methods of production and exchange, the crisis of the old system of values was immediately hidden by recourse to new sublimations, rendered artificially objective by means of the call to the universality of Nature.

5 Le Corbusier, "Urbanisme," *Esprit Nouveau*, Paris 1924 (Eng. trans. *The City of Tomorrow*, 1929. Facsimile edition, MIT Press, Cambridge, Mass., 1971.

Thus Reason and Nature now had to be unified. Enlightenment rationalism could not assume the entire responsibility for the operations that were being carried out, and its practitioners felt the necessity of avoiding a direct confrontation with their own premises.

It is clear that, throughout the eighteenth and early nineteenth centuries, such an ideological cover was encouraged by the contradictions of the *ancien régime*. Incipient urban capitalism was already clashing with those economic structures based on precapitalist exploitation of the soil. It is indicative that the urban theorists did not make this contradiction evident, but rather covered it up, or, better, endeavored to resolve it by relegating the city to the great sea of nature, concentrating all their attention upon the suprastructural aspects of the city.

Urban naturalism, the insertion of the picturesque into the city and into architecture, as the increased importance given to landscape in artistic ideology all tended to negate the now obvious dichotomy between urban reality and the reality of the countryside. They served to prove that there was no disparity between the value acredited to nature and the value acredited to the city as a productive mechanism of new forms of economic accumulation.

The rhetorical and Arcadian naturalism of the seventeenth century was now replaced by a widely persuasive naturalism.

It is, however, important to underline that the deliberate abstraction of Enlightenment theories of the city served only at first to destroy Baroque schemes of city planning and development. At a later date, it served to

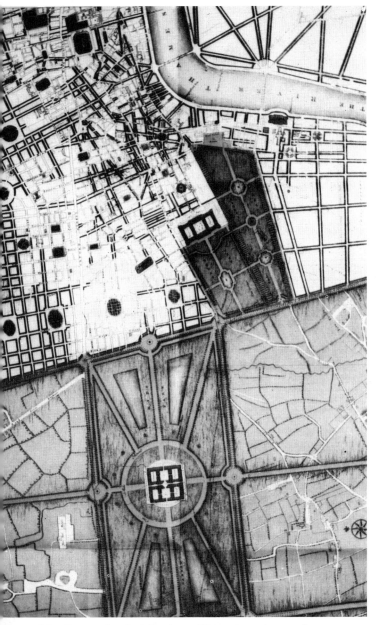

1 John Gwynn, plate from *London and Westminster Improved*, 1776.

discourage, rather than condition, the formation of global models of development. It is therefore not surprising that such a gigantic and avant-garde operation as the reconstruction of Lisbon after the earthquake of 1755 was carried out, under the guidance of the Marquis di Pombal, in a completely empirical spirit, devoid of theoretical abstractions.[6]

Thus, deviating decidedly from Enlightenment criticism in general, architectural thought in the eighteenth and nineteenth centuries played a mostly destructive role. Not having at its disposal a mature substratum of production techniques adequate to the new conditions of bourgeois ideology and economic liberalism, architecture was obliged to restrict its self-criticism to two areas.

1 For polemical reasons architecture exalted everything that could assume an anti-European significance. Piranesi's fragmentation is the consequence of the discovery of that new bourgeois science, historical criticism, but it is also, paradoxically, *criticism of criticism*. The whole fashion of evocations of Gothic, Chinese, and Hindu architecture, and the romantic naturalism of the garden landscape, in which were immersed the jests—devoid of irony—of exotic pavilions and false ruins, are related ideally to the atmosphere of Montesquieu's *Lettres persanes*, Voltaire's *Ingénu* and Leibniz' caustic antioccidentalism. In order to integrate rationalism and criticism, the Europeans confronted their myths with all that which could, by contesting them, confirm their validity. In the romantic English

6 See J.-A. Franca, *Une ville de lumières: la Lisbonne de Pombal*, C.N.R.F., Paris 1965.

garden the time-honored perspective view was nulli-fied. The aggregation of little temple structures, pavil-ions, and grottoes, which seem the meeting places of the most disparate testimonies of human history, signified something other than mere evasion in the fabulous. Rather, the "picturesque" of Brown, Kent, and the Woods, or the "horrid" of Lequeu, made an appeal. By means of an architecture that had already renounced the formation of "objects" to become a *technique of organization of preformed materials*, they asked for an authentication from *outside architecture*. With all the detachment typical of the great critics of the Enlighten-ment, those architects initiated a systematic and fatal autopsy of architecture and all its conventions.

2 Even though its properly formal role had been placed in parentheses by the city, architecture still offered an alternative to the nihilist outlook apparent behind the hallucinating fantasies of Lequeu, Bélanger, or Piranesi. By renouncing a symbolic role, at least in the traditional sense, architecture—in order to avoid destroying itself—discovered its own scientific calling. On one hand, it could become the instrument of social equilibrium, and in this case it was to have to face in full the question of building types—something that was to be done by Durand and Dubut. On the other hand, it could become a science of sensations. This was to be the road pursued by Ledoux, and in a much more system-atic way by Camus de Mézières. The alternatives were thus either the study of the forms assumed by dif-ferent building types, or *architecture parlante*: the same two concepts brought into erupting contrast by Pira-nesi. But, instead of leading to a solution, these con-

cepts were to accentuate architecture's internal crisis throughout the nineteenth century.

Architecture now undertook the task of rendering its work "political." As a political agent the architect had to assume the task of continual invention of advanced solutions, at the most generally applicable level. In the acceptance of this task, the architect's role as idealist became prominent.

The real significance of that utopianism which modern historical study has recognized in Enlightenment architecture is thus laid bare. The truth is that the architectural proposals of eighteenth-century Europe have nothing unrealizable about them. Nor is it accidental that all the vast theorization of the *philosophes* of architecture contains no social utopia to support the urban reformism proclaimed at a purely formal level.

The introduction to the entry on "architecture" written by Quatremère de Quincy for the *Encyclopédie méthodique* is, in fact, a masterpiece of realism, even in the abstract terms in which it is expressed:

Among all the arts, those children of pleasure and necessity, with which man has formed a partnership in order to help him bear the pains of life and transmit his memory to future generations, it can certainly not be denied that *architecture* holds a most outstanding place. Considering it only from the point of view of utility, it surpasses all the arts. It provides for the salubrity of cities, guards the health of men, protects their property, and works only for the safety, repose, and good order of civil life.[7]

Enlightenment realism is, in fact, not even disproved

7 M. Quatremère de Quincy, entry for "architecture," in *Encyclopédie méthodique etc.*, Paris 1778, vol. I, p. 109.

by the gigantic architectural dreams of Boullée or of the pensioners of the *Académie*. The exaltation of scale, the geometric purification, and the ostentatious primitivism—the constant characteristics of these projects —assume concrete significance when read in the light of what the projects really were intended to be: not so much unrealizable dreams, as experimental models of a new method of architectural creation.

From the excessive symbolism of Ledoux or Lequeu to the geometric silence of Durand's formally codified building types, the process followed by Enlightenment architecture is consistent with the new ideological role it had assumed. In order to become part of the structure of the bourgeois city, architecture had to redimension itself, dissolving into the uniformity ensured by preconstituted formal systems.

But this dissolution was not without consequences. It was Piranesi who carried Laugier's theoretical intuitions to their extreme conclusions. His ambiguous evocation of the *Campo Marzio* is the graphic monument of that tentative opening of late Baroque culture to revolutionary ideologies. Just as his *Parere sull-architettura* is its most sensitive literary testimony.[8]

8 See G. B. Piranesi, *Il Campo Marzio dell'antica Roma etc.*, Rome 1761–1762; idem, *Parere su l'architettura*, appended to *Osservazioni etc.*, Rome 1764; W. Körte, "G. B. Piranesi als praktischer Architekt," *Zeitschrift für Kunstgeschichte*, II, 1933; R. Wittkower, "Piranesi's *Parere su l'architettura*," *Journal of the Warburg Institute*, II, 1938–1939, pp. 147–158; U. Vogt-Göknil, *Giovanni Battista Piranesi's "Carceri,"* Origo Verlag, Zurich 1958; P. M. Sekler, "G. B. Piranesi's Carceri: Etchings and Related Drawings," *The Art Quarterly*, XXV, 1962, pp. 331–363; M. Calvesi, introduction to the new edition of H. Focillon, *Piranesi*, Alfa, Bologna 1967; J. Harris, "Le Geay, Piranesi and the International Neo-Classicism in Rome, 1740–1750," in *Essays in the History of Architecture presented to Rudolf Wittkower*, Phaidon Press, London 1967, pp. 189–196; M. G. Messina, "Teoria dell'architettura in G. B. Piranesi," *Controspazio*, 1970, no. 8/9, pp. 6–10 and 1971, no. 6, pp. 20–28; M. Tafuri,

In Piranesi's *Campo Marzio* the late Baroque principle of *variety* is completely rejected. Since Roman antiquity is not only a recollection imbued with nostalgic ideologies and revolutionary expectations, but also a myth to be contested, all forms of classical derivation are treated as mere fragments, as deformed symbols, as hallucinating organisms of an "order" in a state of decay.

Here the order in the details does not produce a simple "tumult in the whole." Rather, it creates a monstrous pullulation of symbols devoid of significance. Like the sadistic atmosphere of his *Carceri*, Piranesi's "forest" demonstrates that it is not only the "sleep of reason" that conjures up monsters, but that even the "wakefulness of reason" can lead to deformation: even if its goal be the Sublime.

Piranesi's critical interpretation of the *Campo Marzio* was not without a prophetic quality. In this work the most advanced point of Enlightenment architecture seems precisely and emphatically to warn of the imminent danger of losing altogether the organic quality of form. It was now the ideal of totality and universality that was in crisis.

Architecture might make the effort to maintain its completeness and preserve itself from total destruction, but such an effort is nullified by the assemblage of architectural pieces in the city. It is in the city that these fragments are pitilessly absorbed and deprived of any autonomy, and this situation cannot be reversed by obstinately forcing the fragments to assume articulated,

"G. B. Piranesi: l'architettura come 'utopia negativa'," *Angelus Novus*, 1971, no. 20, pp. 89–127.

composite configurations. In the *Campo Marzio* we witness an epic representation of the battle waged by architecture against itself. The historically developed language of building types is affirmed here as a superior principle of order, but the configuration of the single building types tends to destroy the very concept of the historically developed language as a whole. History is here invoked as an inherent "value," but Piranesi's paradoxical rejection of historical, archaeological reality makes the civic potential of the total image very doubtful. Formal invention seems to declare its own primacy, but the obsessive reiteration of the inventions reduces the whole organism to a sort of gigantic "useless machine."

Rationalism would seem thus to reveal its own irrationality. In the attempt to absorb all its own contradictions, architectural "reasoning" applies the technique of shock to its very foundations. Individual architectural fragments push one against the other, each indifferent to jolts, while as an accumulation they demonstrate the uselessness of the inventive effort expended on their formal definition.

The archaeological mask of Piranesi's *Campo Marzio* fools no one: this is an experimental design and the city, therefore, remains an unknown. Nor is the act of designing capable of defining new constants of order. This colossal piece of *bricolage* conveys nothing but a self-evident truth: irrational and rational are no longer to be mutually exclusive. Piranesi did not possess the means for translating the dynamic interrelationships of this contradiction into form. He had, therefore, to limit himself to enunciating emphatically that the great new problem was that of the equilibrium of opposites, which in the city finds its appointed place: failure to resolve this problem would mean the destruction of the very concept of architecture.

Essentially it is the struggle between architecture and the city, between the demand for order and the will to formlessness, that assumes epic tone in Piranesi's *Campo Marzio*. Here the "Enlightenment dialectic" on architecture reached an unsurpassed height; but at the same time it reached an ideal tension so violent that it could not be understood as such by Piranesi's contemporaries. Piranesi's excess—as otherwise the excesses of the libertine literature of the era of the *philosophes* —becomes, just through its excessiveness, the revelation of a truth. But the developments of Enlightenment architecture and city planning were quickly to hide that truth.

The unmasking of the contradiction, as an act that in itself might offer a ray of hope for a culture condemned (the expression is Piranesi's)[9] to operate with degraded means, is utilized by Piranesi with remarkable results. And not so much in the formal *bricolage* of the eclectic architectural images of his *Parere* (rather, in this case the contradiction is absorbed and recomposed, and rendered inoffensive), as in his two editions of the *Carceri*.

It is in the *Carceri d'Invenzione*, and in particular the edition of 1760, that Piranesi reveals the consequences of the "loss" announced in his *Campo Marzio*. In the *Carceri* the crisis of *order*, of form, of the classical concept of *Stimmung*, assumes "social" connotations. Here

9 G. B. Piranesi, *Parere su l'architettura*, p. 2.

2 Giovanni Battista Piranesi, plate from *Campo Marzio dell'antica Roma*, 1761–1762. Perspective view of the area of Hadrian's tomb and the *Bustum Hadriani*.

the destruction of the very concept of space merges with a symbolic allusion to the new condition being created by a radically changing society. (Piranesi's "Romanity" is always matched by an awareness and concern that is European.) In these etchings the space of the building—the prison—is an infinite space. What has been destroyed is the center of that space, signifying the correspondence between the collapse of ancient values, of the ancient order, and the "totality" of the disorder. *Reason*, the author of this destruction—a destruction felt by Piranesi to be fatal—is transformed into irrationality. But the prison, precisely because infinite, coincides with the space of human existence. This is very clearly indicated by the hermetic scenes Piranesi designs within the mesh of lines of his "impossible" compositions. Thus what we see in the *Carceri* is only the new existential condition of human collectivity, liberated and condemned at the same time by its own reason. And Piranesi translates into images not a reactionary criticism of the social promises of the Enlightenment, but a lucid prophecy of what society, liberated from the ancient values and their consequent restraints, will have to be.

By now there is no other possibility than that of global, voluntary alienation in collective form. Constriction is the new law that it is absurd to question. Resistance to this new law is paid for with torture. Note the scene of torture inserted in plate II of the *Carceri*. It is not without significance that the tortured person is drawn as a superhuman being, around whom gathers an indistinct mass. In the totally alienated society the sixteenth- and seventeenth-century libertine has no longer any escape. His "heroism" is condemned with indifference even by Piranesi.[10]

With Piranesi the experience of anguish makes its first appearance in modern form. In the *Carceri* we are already in the presence of an anguish generated by the anonymity of the person and the "silence of things."

It seems evident also that for Piranesi this silence coincides with a formal expression of "signs." After the eclipse of the Rococo in his four *Capricci* of 1741, his images and forms are reduced to empty signs. Eloquent testimony of this is the pure sphere of his altar in Santa Maria del Priorato.

But a universe of empty signs is a place of total disorder. The only course left will be to utilize as a new system that which in Piranesi's work is anguished anticipation. What is negative in Piranesi will reemerge in the architectural experience of the Enlightenment only from time to time, as a sudden resurgence of a remote guilt complex.

The inherent ambiguity and disorder of the city, which toward the middle of the eighteenth century was assuming a new representative role in national economies (even if the structural relationship between city and country was to be revolutionized only much later), was the prevailing concept in the greater part of eighteenth-century planning. But it is very difficult to find, in the work of the Woods, Palmer, the Adams, George

10 Lopez-Rey has observed that in Piranesi's *Carceri* the figures are present more to allow the instruments of torture to function than to communicate the horror of torture. It is this same author who has recognized a contrast between the work of Piranesi and that of Goya. See J. Lopez-Rey, "Las Cárceles de Piranesi, los prisoneros de Goya," in *Scritti di Storia dell'Arte in onore di Lionello Venturi*, De Luca, Rome 1956, vol. II, pp. 111–116.

Dance, Jr., Karl Ludwig Engel, or L'Enfant, any consciousness of that significance Piranesi gave to the *eclipse of form* as demonstrated in the city.

The fragmentation introduced into city planning at an ideological level by Laugier was, however, revived in the eclectic theorization of Milizia, who, almost paraphrasing Laugier, wrote:

A city is like a forest, thus the distribution of a city is like that of a park. There must be squares, crossroads, and straight and spacious streets in great numbers. But this is not enough. It is necessary that the plan be designed with taste and vivacity of spirit, so that it has both order and fantasy, eurythmy and variety: streets laid out here in star formation, there in a claw pattern, in one part in herring-bone plan, in another like a fan, and further on parallel, and everywhere intersections of three or four streets in different positions, with a multitude of public squares, all different in size, shape, and decoration.[11]

In Milizia's next proposal for the city no one can fail to see the influence of a cultivated sensualism:

He who does not know how to vary our pleasures will never give us pleasure. [The city] should in fact be a varied picture of infinite unexpected episodes, a great order in the details, confusion, uproar and tumult in the whole.

Milizia continues:

The plan of the city should be distributed in such a way

11 F. Milizia, *Principi di architettura civile*, 3rd ed., Bassano 1813, vol. II, pp. 26–27. This passage, as indeed Milizia's whole treatise, is a plagarism: he merely paraphrases Laugier's ideas. But his text is of interest as testimony of the diffusion of the theory of the "naturalistic city" in the course of the eighteenth century.

that the magnificence of the whole is subdivided in an infinity of individual beauties, all so different one from the other that the same object is never encountered twice, and moving from one end to the other one finds in each quarter something new, unique, and surprising. Order must reign, but in a kind of confusion ... and from a multitude of regular parts the whole must give a certain idea of irregularity and chaos, which is so fitting to great cities.[12]

Order and chaos, regularity and irregularity, organic structure and the lack of organic structure. Here certainly we have come a long way from the late Baroque precept of *unity in variety*, which in Shaftsbury had assumed a mystic connotation.

The control of a reality lacking organic structure, achieved by operating on that very lack, not in order to give it structure but, rather, to draw forth from it a whole complex of coexisting meanings: this is what the writings of Laugier, Piranesi, Milizia and—later and in more moderate tone—those of Quatremère de Quincy introduced into architectural thought.

But in opposition to these ideas there were soon pleas for a traditional adherence to rules. Giovanni Antolini, in commenting upon Milizia's *Principî*, did not fail to lash out against the intuitions of Milizia's theories, and to defend Vitruvian authority and Galiani's ideal exemplification of it. Opposing the exaltation of empiricism and the picturesque of the Woods, of Palmer's Bath, of the Edinburgh Cresents and the 1807 plan for Milan, were the rationalist strictness of Gwynn's pro-

12 *Ibid.*, p. 28.

ject for London, Muratti's for Bari, and the new plans for Saint Petersburg and Helsinki.

Of special interest for the purpose of our analysis is the opposition of ideals demonstrated by Antolini's stand against the Commission of 1807 for the Napoleonic plan for Milan.

The members of the Commission were disposed to operate within the structural terms of the city as it had developed historically, except that they pronounced an explicit judgment on that development. As a product of power and events determined by prejudice, myth, the feudal system, and the forces of the Counter-Reformation, the whole historic structure of the Lombard capital was for them something to be made rational, to be clarified in its functions and forms. It was also something to be treated in such a way that from the encounter between the old preexisting parts—places representative of obscurantism—and the newly reordered and rebuilt areas—places representative of the light of the Enlightenment—there might emerge a clear and unequivocal hypothesis concerning the future and physical structure of the city.

It is not by chance that Antolini took an opposing view in regard to the Napoleonic plan. If the Commission was disposed to some extent to establish rapport with the historic city, toning down the ideology of its own interventions in relation to it, Antolini refused any such give and take. His design for the Foro Bonaparte is at one and the same time a radical alternative to the history of the city and a symbol full of absolute ideological values, a place in the city that seems to present the sum of the whole and aims at changing the entire

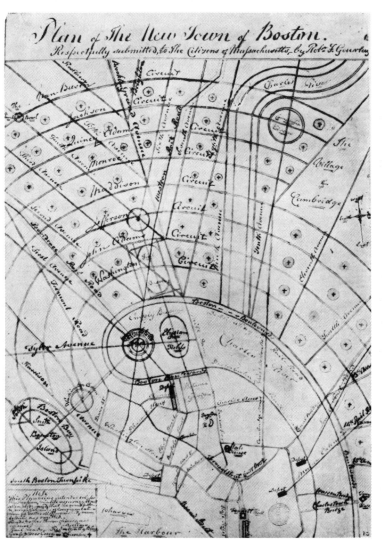

3 Fleming Gourlay, original plan for the Back Bay in Boston, 1844.

urban structure by restoring to architecture a communicative role of peremptory character.[13]

The antithesis is complete. It involves the whole way of considering the communicative role of the city. For the Commission of 1807 the protagonist of the new ideal and functional message was the urban structure as such. For Antolini, on the contrary, the restructuring of the city was accomplished by introducing into the network of its contradictory values a clamorously disruptive urban place, capable of radiating induced effects that reject any contaminating influence. For him the city as a system of communications was summed up in the absolute, peremptory "message."

The two roads of modern art and architecture are here already delineated. It is, in fact, the inherent opposition within all modern art: those who search into the very bowels of reality in order to know and assimilate its values and wretchedness; and those who desire to go beyond reality, who want to construct *ex novo* new realities, new values, and new public symbols.

What divides the Napoleonic Commission from Antolini is the same difference that separates Monet from Cézanne, Munch from Braque, Raoul Hausmann from Mondrian, Häring from Mies, or Rauschenberg from Vasarely.

Between Laugier's "forest" and Antolini's aristocratic reserve, however, there existed a third road, destined to lead to a new way of operating upon and controlling urban form. L'Enfant's plan for Washington, or

13 See G. Antolini, *Descrizione del Foro Bonaparte, presentato coi disegni al comitato di governo della Repubblica Cisalpina etc.*, Milan 1802; A. Rossi, "Il concetto di tradizione nell'architettura neoclassica milanese," *Società*, XII, 1956, no. 2, pp. 474–493; G. Mezzanotte, *L'architettura neoclassica in Lombardia*, Esi, Naples 1966.

those for Jeffersonville, Jackson, and Missouri City inspired by Jefferson's theories of city planning, use means that were new with respect to European models.[14]

It must here be emphasized that in eighteenth-century America naturalistic ideology found a properly political field of development. It was indeed Jefferson who, with extreme lucidity, recognized the institutional and pedagogical value of architecture.

For Jefferson the utilization of classicism, Palladianism, and English experimentalism[15] was nothing other than the demonstration of the fact that, with the American Revolution, the reason of the European Enlightenment became the practical guide to the "construction of democracy." With greater effectiveness than any European protagonist of politically committed art, Jefferson carried out his role as organizer of culture, having the opportunity to do so in "official" works. This is the role he repeatedly played as consultant in the planning of Washington, in the designing of the White House and the Capitol, and in the restoration of the Governor's Mansion in Williamsburg, and in his architectural activity in general.[16]

14 On Jefferson's activity as city planner see J. W. Reps, "Thomas Jefferson's Checkerboard Towns," in *Journal of the Society of Architectural Historians*, XX, 1961, no. 3, pp. 108—114.
15 For the influence on Jefferson's architecture of the writings of Robert Morris (R. Morris, *Select Architecture*, London 1755), see C. Lancaster, "Jefferson's Indebtedness to Robert Morris," *Journal of the Society of Architectural Historians*, X, 1951, no. 1, pp. 2—10, and T. H. Waterman, "Thomas Jefferson. His Early Works in Architecture," *Gazette des Beaux-Arts*, XXIV, 1943, no. 918, pp. 89—106.
16 On Jefferson as architect see F. Kimball, *Thomas Jefferson Architect*, Boston 1916, reprinted by Da Capo Press, New York 1968; I. T. Frary, *Thomas Jefferson, Architect and Builder*, Garret and Massie, Richmond 1939; F.D. Nichols, *Thomas Jefferson's Architectural Drawings*, Massachusetts Historical Society, Memorial Foundation, University of Virginia Press, 1961; J.S. Acker-

To be considered as an integral part of Jefferson's architectural ideas and undertakings is his agrarian and antiurban politics.

Hamilton interpreted the aims of the political situation—that had begun with the American Revolution—to be economic, and coldly and lucidly pursued an accelerated development of American financial and industrial capital. Jefferson, on the contrary, remained faithful to a democracy arrested at the level of a utopia.

Agricultural economy, local and regional autonomy as pivots of the democratic system, and the restraining of industrial development all had an explicit significance for Jefferson. They were symbols of his fear in face of the processes set in motion by the Revolution. Essentially this was fear of the dangers of involution, of the transformation of democracy into a new authoritarianism, brought into being by capitalist competition, urban development, and the birth and growth of an urban proletariat.

In this sense Jefferson was against the city and against the development of industrial economy. This is why he tried to impede the logical economic consequences of democracy.

With him came into being "radical America," or rather the *ambiguous conscience* of American intellectuals, who acknowledge the foundations of the democratic system while opposing its concrete manifestations.

Seen in this light Jefferson's democracy was again a

man, "Il presidente Jefferson e il palladianismo americano," *Bollettino del centro studi A. Palladio*, VI, 1964, part II, pp. 39—48. For a complete bibliography up to 1959 see W. B. O'Neal, *A Checklist of Writings on Thomas Jefferson as an Architect*, American Association of Architectural Biographers, 1959.

utopia, but no longer of the vanguard; rather, it was a utopia of the rear guard. (In passing we may note the ideological affinity between Jefferson and Frank Lloyd Wright, discussed by such critics as Fitch and Scully.)[17]

Agrarian democracy had therefore to honor itself. Monticello, the villa farmhouse designed and built by Jefferson for himself in several stages (from about 1769 on), is a monument to agrarian utopia. At Monticello the models of Palladio, Scamozzi, and Morris are used pragmatically. In place of laterally attached pavilions are two terrace-roofed service wings that converge upon the residential nucleus, which stands out in its guise of a villa-temple. But worked into the geometric scheme are a whole series of technological and functional inventions, which reveal the architect's intention of integrating classicism with "modern" necessities, of demonstrating all the possibilities for the concrete civil and social uses of classicism. (It has been noted, for example, that at Monticello, with its clear distinction of spaces for service and served, Jefferson anticipated something that was to be typical of Wright and Kahn.)

Jefferson further developed his program in other architectural works. In the designs for the houses of Battersea, Farmington in Kentucky[18], and Poplar Forest—following a syntax that Lancaster has recognized as

17 See J. M. Fitch, "Architecture of Democracy: Jefferson and Wright," in *Architecture and the Esthetics of Plenty*, Columbia University Press, New York—London 1961, p. 31 ff.; V. Scully, *American Architecture and Urbanism*, Thames and Hudson, London 1969; *idem*, "American Houses: Thomas Jefferson to Frank Lloyd Wright," in *The Rise of an American Architecture*, Metropolitan Museum of Art, New York, and Pall Mall Press, London 1970, p. 163 ff.
18 See F. Kimball, "Jefferson's Designs for Two Kentucky Houses," *Journal of the Society of Architectural Historians*, IX, 1950, no. 3, pp. 14—16.

deriving from the study of Morris's graphic works[19]
—he used a combined geometry of compound and intersecting polygons. Jefferson thus anticipated the reduction to a purely geometric (and therefore completely antisymbolic) language that was to be the final stage of Enlightenment architecture in Europe (see the didactic works of Durand and Dubut).

The heroic aspect of classicism was accepted by Jefferson as a European myth to be "made" American (and for this reason it could be used with freedom and open-mindedness). But when this heroic aspect was presented as *value*, as *constructed reason*, as a quality capable of unifying the divergent ideals of the composite society of the young United States, it had also to be presented as an accessible, diffusible, social value.

The utopia of Jefferson the architect is fully expressed in the "domestic heroism" of his classicism. The *values* (read: images of Reason) were imported from Europe already elaborated in all their weighty solemnity, but they were immediately stripped of anything that might isolate them from civil life. In other words, they were deprived of their aura of inaccessibility.

In this respect it is interesting to see how Jefferson worked in designing the new Capitol of Richmond. With the consultation of the French architect Clérisseau—Jefferson was in France in 1784—he reworked the model of the Maison Carrée in Nîmes, changing only the order of the exterior columns (from Corinthian to Ionic), and sent the drawing to America. Thus the Rich-

19 C. Lancaster, *op. cit.*

mond Capitol was a building *ready-made* in Europe, adapted to glorify the new democratic institutions made "sacred" by this *social temple*, which became a constantly referred to and repeated model (see Th. Walter's Girard College, Latrobe's Bank of Pennsylvania at Philadelphia, the works of Strickland, etc.).

Thus a fusion was attempted between the new and the completely empirical vision of antiquity. Jefferson proposed to keep alive that "resurrection of the dead" —to use the words of Marx[20]—utilized by the European Enlightenment in response to the crisis posed by the French Revolution. This is very clear in his design for the University of Virginia at Charlottesville (1817–1826), in which he availed himself of the consultation of Thorton and Latrobe. The university campus, according to the Jeffersonian statute, must be an "academic village": his agrarian ideology thoroughly imbues the pedagogical program. Organized on an open "U" scheme, converging on the central domed library, the university is divided into a series of individual pavilions—self-sufficient didactic nuclei, complete with academic residences, joined together by a continuous portico. In the formal organization, order and liberty seek their integration. On the one hand, the pavilions, all different from one another, demonstrate the extreme flexibility of the classical models. (And it is significant that the walls dividing the gardens, placed between the didactic nuclei and the residences, are given an undulating form, astonishing for its formal liberty.) On the other hand, the general plan and the

20 From K. Marx and F. Engels, *1848 in Germany and France.*

strictness of the concluding rotunda explicitly allude to the stability, permanence, and absoluteness of the institution.

Jefferson thus produced the first eloquent image of what was to be the most dramatic effort of the intellectuals of "radical America": reconciliation of the mobility of values with the stability of principles, the individual impulse—always stimulated to the point of anarchy or neurosis—with the social dimension. This was exactly the unresolved contradiction that de Tocqueville was to point out, in his *Démocratie en Amérique* (1835—1840), as the danger overhanging the new democratic order.

It is true that Jefferson's agrarian ideology presupposed great optimism and was thoroughly opposed to any polemical doubt. But certainly by his time, in regard to architecture and city planning, such an ideology could not be impervious to the fact that the only correct way to "use" the European ideology of Reason was to recognize that utopia (architectural classicism or antifederal and antiurban democracy) could no longer be a creation of the vanguard. This is completely evident in the history of the planning of Washington and the development of the City Beautiful movement.

In the planning of Washington, the Jeffersonian ideological program was immediately taken up by L'Enfant. The founding of a capital translates the "foundation of a new world" into visual terms, and corresponds to a unitary decision and a "free choice" that no collective will in Europe had been able to put forward. Seen in this light, the form of the new city logically assumes primary and predominant significance. The political

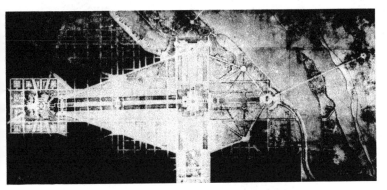

4 *Top*, view of Washington from the south bank of the Anacostia River, 1843. *Center and bottom*, perspective view and plan of the Senate Park Commission's design for the center of Washington, 1902.

choice that had been made had to be expressed by appropriating the available European models. Or, rather, these models had to be grafted onto the American tradition of city planning. L'Enfant intentionally superimposed the scheme of the colonial grid and a scheme —very advanced for its time—developed from Le Nôtre's French garden, Wren's plan for the city of London, eighteenth-century Karlsruhe, and Patte's fantastic Paris.

The city in L'Enfant's Washington is really *new nature.* The models derived from the Europe of absolutism and despotism are now expropriated by the capital of democratic institutions, and translated into a social dimension certainly unknown at the Versailles of Louis XIV. (It is also significant that, while the plan for Washington was actually realized, Wren's city, for lack of administrative instrumentation, remained but a cultural proposition.)

In Washington, the ferment already stirring in the seventeenth-century plans for Annapolis and Savannah could now be integrated one with the other and raised to a level of eloquence for the eyes of the world, not the least for the physical dimensions of the undertaking. Within the double network of orthogonal and radial roads (of the urban forest—i.e., of nature made into an object of civic use) fifteen nodes of development are created by the fifteen public squares, allegories of the fifteen states of the Union. At the same time the division between legislative and executive power is given concrete expression in the "L" structure of the two main axes leading out from the White House and the Capitol and intersecting at the Washington Monument. (The latter originally designed as an obelisk-*cum*-colonnade by Robert Mills, the architect of the Treasury Building, but in the end realized in the simpler—more "metaphysical," we might say—form of an obelisk alone.) The connection between the two functional and symbolic poles of the new capital is provided by the oblique artery of Pennsylvania Avenue.[21]

After L'Enfant's dismissal, provoked by the despotic control he presumed to wield over the developments of the city (and here it should be noted that, from the beginning, Jefferson was against the grandiloquence of the French architect's plan), Washington began its life. By 1800 it numbered three thousand inhabitants. European travelers, such as Trollope and Dickens, admired it. But the new city was still a compromise between the antiurban ideology of Jefferson—forgotten by the statesman only momentarily in order to create a symbolic place in which the idea of the Union could be completely expressed—and the *grandeur* of L'Enfant. The broad openness of the plan is balanced by firmly defined points which structure its image. It is not by mere chance that the least economically necessary city in America is also the most "configured."

The fact is that, in its timelessness, the classicism that dominates the city's form, development, and monumental places corresponds to Jefferson's ideological

21 On the history of the planning of Washington see the well-documented work by J. W. Reps, *Monumental Washington. The Planning and Development of the Capital Center*, Princeton University Press, Princeton 1967, reviewed by S.M. Sherman in *Journal of the Society of Architectural Historians*, XXVIII, 1969, no. 2, pp. 145–148. See also E. Peets, "The Geneology of the Plan of Washington," in *ibid.*, X, 1951, no. 2, pp. 3–4, and the two volumes by C. M. Green, *Washington: Village and Capital, 1800–1878* and *Washington: Capital City, 1879–1950*, Princeton University Press, Princeton 1962 and 1963.

program. In Washington, the nostalgic evocation of European values was concentrated in the capital of a society whose drive to economic and industrial development was leading to the concrete and intentional destruction of those values.

Washington thus constitutes a sort of American "bad conscience," which, however, can exist undisturbed alongside the iron-clad laws of industrial development. What makes this passive duplicity possible is that the city is a monument; as a monument it is free to demonstrate continually and openly its own untimeliness.

This is why, after the unsuccessful attempts at a naturalistic and romantic definition of the Mall by the landscape architect Andrew Jackson Downing (1850 and after), and after the more realistic speculative initiatives of Alexander Robey Shepherd (from 1871 to 1873), who tried to introduce into the plan the dilated dimensions of Hausmann's Paris, and after the projects of Theodore Bingham, Samuel Parsons, Jr., and Cass Gilbert for Potomac Park and the Mall (1900), finally the Park Commission, with significantly suprahistorical continuity, took up again L'Enfant's original idea and carried it to conclusion.

The Park Commission, formed in 1900 by Senator McMillan, with the advice of his secretary Charles Moore, was made up of Daniel Burnham, Charles McKim, and Frederick Law Olmsted, Jr. Their model was still "academic" Europe. Indeed, Burnham and his colleagues made a long trip to study the plans of Vienna, Budapest, Paris, Rome, Frankfurt, and London. All the programs of the City Beautiful movement were poured into the heart of Washington. It is, in fact, to this project that those programs were really suitable. The Park Commission had not to complete a city created and adapted to business; rather, it had to work with a deliberately abstract collective symbol, an ideology realized in terms of urban images, the allegory of a political organization whose socioeconomic consequence is a rapid and mobile evolution but which here wishes to present itself immobile in its principles. The city of Washington gives form to the immobility and conventionality of those principles, there represented as ahistoric. New York, Chicago, and Detroit are left to be the protagonists of development. (And this is true even if Burnham and the City Beautiful planners tried to interpret the new dimension of those cities in terms of a formal quality. What Burnham and the others were actually doing was anticipating, at a very abstract and ingenuous suprastructural level, the need for unitary control over development.)

The Park Commission's design for the Mall was exhibited in 1902, and aroused enormous interest on the part of the public. Even in the project stage it realized its objective: to give concrete expression to the United States, to create the symbol *par excellence* of the will of the people that had given life to the Union. The two perspectives *ad infinitum* converging on the area of the Washington Monument—very suitably arranged with a series of terraces—were concluded by the Lincoln and Jefferson memorials, the first by Henry Bacon, begun in 1912, and the second carried out *ca.* 1930 (architects: J. Russell Pope, followed by Eggers and Higgins). The Park Commission's plan and the two memorials (the plan for the definitive arrangement of Pennsylvania

Avenue was to be presented only in 1964 by the firm of Skidmore, Owings, and Merrill) are eloquent testimony to the principles guiding the task of their authors.

The classicism that informs them is complete, not mediated or compromised as in the academic architecture of Europe in the period between 1920 and 1940. Without inhibitions these designs demonstrate that, for the ideal of the Union, history has come to a standstill. In their enormous scale these works simply do not attempt to relate to the individual. The only thing of interest here is the public, social, world dimension. *Reason become democracy* must enunciate to the world the abstract principles of the *pax Americana*.

This explains why—in 1902 as well as in the 1930s or 1960s—the accomplishments of avant-garde architecture and city planning were rejected for the capital of the United States. Washington tends to underscore in every way its own separation (not its extraneousness) from development. In it, as in a timeless, indisputable, completely "positive" Olympus, is concentrated the anxiety of America in search of roots.

Thus the representation of the stability of values can show itself for what it is. That is to say, a conventional but real aspiration, which must be satisfied by keeping it carefully separated from the forces of development, from technology's continual revolutionizing modernity.

Values, stability, and form are thus presented as objects that are unreal but have nonetheless taken material form. They are symbols of the American longing for *something other than itself*, terms of reference for a society continually terrified by the processes it has itself set in motion and indeed considers irreversible. Classicism, as an ideal of uncontaminated Reason, is thus consciously presented in all its regressive character. This is what has taken place in Washington all through the century. But it also happens in a less obvious way everywhere in America, coming to a head in what Kallmann has defined as an architecture of "compositional rigorists"—of Louis Kahn, of Kallmann himself, of Giurgola and Johansen—who between 1950 and 1960 could present their aspirations to form as an evasive expression of "anticonsumerism." The bad conscience of radical America, from Jefferson to Kahn, turns in upon itself in pathetic homage to inoperative values.

But just the opposite of the case of Washington is that of New York. The pragmatic scheme of development of New York, as planned by the Commission of 1811, has so frequently been analyzed for its relationship with the value structure typical of American society from its beginnings, that we need not reexamine it here.[22]

22 See L. Benevolo, *Storia dell'architettura moderna*, 4th ed., Laterza, Bari 1971, and M. Manieri-Elia, *L'architettura del dopoguerra in USA*, Cappelli, Bologna 1966. Concerning the plan of 1807—1811 for the city of New York, Manieri-Elia writes, "It seems that on the urban scale the puritan and "antiarchitectural" attitude coincides perfectly with the sense of Jeffersonian libertarian individualism, whose governmental system, as is very evident in the Declaration of Independence, is the least obtrusive possible functional support. If the government must be but an elastic instrument, modifiable at any moment to serve inalienable human rights, all the more reason for a city plan to guarantee the maximum elasticity and present the minimum resistance to productive initiative." (*op. cit.*, pp. 64—66). See, in addition, the exceptional documentation on the formation of American cities in J. W. Reps, *The Making of Urban America*, Princeton University Press, Princeton 1965. On Washington as a striking example of continuity between Enlightenment ideology and the Europeanism of the City Beautiful movement in America between 1893 and 1920, see: J. W. Reps, *Monumental Washington, cit.* See also, A. Fein, "The American City: the Ideal and the Real," in *The Rise of an American Architec-*

From as early as the mid-eighteenth century, the great historical merit of American city planning has been the considering of the problem explicitly from the point of view of those forces which provoke morphological change in the city, and controlling them with a pragmatic attitude completely foreign to European practice.

The use of a regular network of arteries as a simple, flexible support for an urban structure to be safeguarded in its continual transformation, realizes an objective never arrived at in Europe. In the American city, absolute liberty is granted to the single architectural fragment, but this fragment is situated in a context that it does not condition formally: the secondary elements of the city are given maximum articulation, while the laws governing the whole are rigidly maintained.

Thus urban planning and architecture are finally separated. The geometric character of the plan of Washington, as earlier that of Philadelphia and later that of New York, does not seek an architectural correspondence in the forms of the single buildings. Unlike what happens in Saint Petersburg or Berlin, architecture is free to explore the most diverse expressions. The urban system assumes only the task of stating the degree to which figurative liberty may be exploited or, better, of guaranteeing, with its own formal rigidity, a stable reference of dimension. The urban structures of American cities thus opened the way to an incredible richness of expression that, particularly after the

ture, cit., pp. 51–112, and the essay by M. Manieri Elia, "Per una città 'imperiale.' Daniel H. Burnham e il movimento City Beautiful," in the volume by G. Ciucci, F. Dal Co, M. Manieri-Elia, and M. Tafuri, *La città americana dalla Guerra Civile al New Deal*, Laterza, Bari 1973.

OLMSTED'S
Sketch Map
OF
BUFFALO
Showing the relation of the
Park System
TO THE
ENERAL PLAN OF THE CITY.

5 Frederick Law Olmsted, plan of Buffalo showing the relation of the
park system to the general plan of urban development, 1876.

mid-nineteenth century, was deposited in their free and open networks. We might say metaphorically that the ethic of free-trade here encountered the pioneering spirit.

2 Form as Regressive Utopia

What our brief analysis of the experiences and intuited preconceptions of eighteenth-century architecture has laid bare is the crisis of the traditional concept of *form*, a crisis which arose precisely through the growing awareness of the city as an autonomous field of architectural intervention. (Our historical excursus into the development of Washington has provided a perfect illustration of this situation.)

Enlightenment architecture from the very beginning postulated one of the concepts fundamental to the development of contemporary art: the disarticulation of form and the antiorganic quality of structure. Nor is it without significance that the institution of these new formal qualities was from the first related to the problem of the new city, which was about to become the institutional locus of modern bourgeois society.

The solicitations of theorists for a revision of formal principles did not, however, lead to a real revolution of meaning but, rather, to an acute crisis of values. In the course of the nineteenth century, the new dimensions presented by the problem of the industrial city made the crisis only more acute, with the result that art was to have difficulty in finding any suitable road by which to follow the developments of urban reality.

On the other hand, the breaking asunder of the organic character of form was completely concentrated in the architectural operation, without finding an outlet in the urban dimension. When we observe a "piece" of Victorian architecture we are struck by the over-wroughtness of the "object." All too rarely do we consider that, for nineteenth-century architects, eclecticism and plurality of expression was the proper answer to the multiple disintegrative stimuli induced by the new physical environment configured by technology's "universe of precision."

The fact that architecture could respond to that "universe of precision" with nothing more than an "approximation" is not surprising. It was in reality the urban structure, precisely in its registration of the conflicts created by that victory of technological progress, that had radically changed. The city had become an open structure, within which it was utopian to seek points of equilibrium.

But architecture, at least as traditionally conceived, is a stable structure, which gives form to permanent values and consolidates urban morphology.

Those wishing to give up this traditional conception and bind architecture instead to the destiny of the city, had only to regard the city as the specific place of technological production—and the city itself as a technological product—thus reducing architecture to a mere link in the production chain. Piranesi's prophecy of the bourgeois city as an "absurd machine" was, in a certain way, actually realized in the metropolises organized in the nineteenth century as primary structures of the capitalist economy.

The zoning governing the development of those metropolises made no effort—at first—to hide its class character. The ideologists of radical or humanitarian convictions were indeed free to exhibit the irrationality of the industrial city. But this they could do only by forgetting (and not just incidentally) that this irrationality was such only for an observer disposed to delude himself of being *au dessus de la mêlée*. Humanitarian utopianism and radical criticism had an unexpected effect: they convinced the bourgeoisie to examine for themselves this problem of the accord between rationality and irrationality.

For all that has been said, it will be seen that this problem is intrinsic to the formation of the urban ideology. And in the abstract, it is familiar to all the figurative arts of the nineteenth century, since the very origin of romantic eclecticism was the redemption of ambiguity as a critical value in itself: exactly that ambiguity pushed to the extreme by Piranesi.

What had allowed Piranesi to mediate the terrifying prophecy of the eclipse of the sacred, with primitivistic nostalgia and flights into the sublime, is also what allowed romantic eclecticism to make itself the interpreter of the merciless commercialization of the human environment, by immersing in it particles of completely worn-out values, presented in all their contorted muteness and falsity, as if to demonstrate that no subjective effort can regain an authenticity lost forever.

Nineteenth-century ambiguity consists wholly in the unrestrained exhibition of a false conscience, which attempts an ultimate ethical redemption by displaying its own lack of authenticity. If the eclectic taste for collecting forms the stylistic expression of this ambiguity, the city is its field of application.

In order to attempt this redemption, Impressionist painting had to take its place in an observatory situated within the urban environment, but far removed from the real meaning of that environment by virtue of subtle observational deformations that merely simulated an objective scientific detachment.

The first political responses to this situation centered on regaining a traditional utopianism, which the Enlightenment seemed to have done away with. But the specific responses of the methods of visual communication introduced a new type of utopianism: the utopia implicit in the realized facts, in the concreteness of "things" constructed and verifiable.

For this reason the utopian trend in nineteenth-century politics was to have only very indirect relationships with the ideas of the "modern movement." Indeed, those relationships, which have been recognized for the most part by present-day historians, between the utopias of Fourier, Owen, and Cabet and the theoretical models of Unwin, Geddes, Howard, or Stein, on the one hand, and those of the Garnier-Le Corbusier current, on the other, are but suppositions in need of careful verification. It is likely that these relationships will come to be considered as functional and as forming part of the same phenomena one wishes to analyze by means of them.[23]

23 It is not possible to treat with a similar set of criteria both utopian socialism and its proposals for urban reorganization, and the ideological formation of the modern movement. One can only note the alternative role played by utopian romanticism in respect to those ideologies. But its developments, particularly the practice of Anglo-Saxon planning, should be compared with the models

6 The Crystal Palace, London, 1851, seen in a nineteenth-century engraving.

It is clear, however, that the specific responses of Marxist criticism to the problem around which utopian thought was obliged to turn incessantly had two immediate consequences for the formation of new urban ideologies:

1 By again considering the general problems in strictly structural terms, it made evident the checkmate to which utopia condemned itself, revealing the secret will to arrive at the brink of destruction implicit in the utopian hypothesis.

2 By doing away with the romantic dream of a mere incidence of subjective action on the destiny of society, the fact that the very concept of destiny is a creation stemming from the new relationships of production became clear to bourgeois thought. As a sublimation of real phenomena, the *courageous acceptance* of destiny—a fundamental of the bourgeois ethic—was able to redeem the misery and impoverishment which that "destiny" itself had induced at all levels of civil life, and above all in its archform: the city.

The end of utopianism and the birth of realism are not distinct moments within the process of ideological formation of the "modern movement." Rather, beginning in the fourth decade of the nineteenth century, realistic utopianism and utopian realism overlap and complement one another. The decline of the social utopia sanctioned ideology's surrender to the *politics of*

elaborated by the New Deal. On the significance of the *ideology of work*, that within the socialist tradition so strongly influenced the rise and development of nineteenth- and early twentieth-century theories of city planning, see the fundamental article by M. Cacciari, "Utopia e socialismo," *Contropiano*, 1970, no. 3, pp. 563–686. See also, by the same author, *Sul problema dell'organizzazione. Germania 1917–1921, introduzione a György Lukács, Kommunismus 1920–21*, Marsilio, Padua 1972.

7 *Top*, design by Building Corporation of London for workmen's housing, 1865. *Bottom*, Louis H. Sullivan, theoretical design for a city with tiered skyscrapers, from *The Graphic*, V, Dec. 19, 1891. The drawing by Sullivan illustrates his article on the advantages of a regulation of the height of commercial buildings.

things brought about by the laws of profit. Architectural, artistic, and urban ideology was left with the *utopia of form* as a way of recovering the human totality through an ideal synthesis, as a way of embracing disorder through order.

Being directly related to the reality of production, architecture was not only the first to accept, with complete lucidity, the consequences of its own commercialization, but was even able to put this acceptance into effect before the mechanisms and theories of political economy had furnished the instruments for such a task. Starting from its own specific problems, modern architecture as a whole had the means to create an ideological situation ready to fully integrate design, at all levels, with the reorganization of production, distribution, and consumption in the new capitalist city.

Analyzing the course of the modern movement as an ideological instrument from the second half of the nineteenth century up to 1931, the date in which the crisis was felt in all sectors and at all levels, means tracing a history divided into three successive phases:

(a) a first, which witnesses the formation of urban ideology as an overcoming of late romantic mythology;

(b) a second, which sees the task of the artistic avant-garde develop as the creation of ideological projects and the individualization of "unsatisfied needs," which are then consigned for concrete resolution to architecture (painting, poetry, music, and sculpture being able to realize this objective on but a purely ideal level);

(c) a third, in which architectural ideology becomes *ideology of the plan*. This phase is in turn put in crisis and supplanted when, after the crisis of 1929, with the

elaboration of the anticyclical theories and the international reorganization of capital, and after the launching in Russia of the First Five-Year Plan, architecture's ideological function seems to be rendered superfluous, or limited to rear-guard tasks of marginal importance.

My intention in the following pages is merely to set forth the main lines of this process, emphasizing but a few of the principal events, in order to furnish a framework for future elaborations and more detailed analyses.

3 Ideology and Utopia

It is now necessary to define more carefully the conditions of intellectual work in general at the moment of formation of the modern bourgeois ideologies and at the moment these ideologies are overcome.

Ultimately the problem is that of evaluating the significance given in the early part of our century to *utopia as a project*.

Without such an analysis the sense of the entire cycle of modern architecture is incomprehensible.

Why is it that all the "tragedy" of the great nineteenth-century *Kultur*, and all the utopia of Weimar, could not survive except by seeking complete dominion over the future?

The unproductiveness of intellectual work was the crime that weighed upon the conscience of the cultural world of the nineteenth century, and which advanced ideologies had to overcome. To turn ideology into utopia thus became imperative. In order to survive, ideology had to negate itself as such, break its own crystallized forms, and throw itself entirely into the "construction of the future." This revision of ideology was thus a project for establishing the dominion of a *realized ideology* over the forms of development.

Weber, Scheler, Pareto, Mannheim: at the beginning

of the twentieth century, the unmasking of the idols that obstructed the way to a global rationalization of the productive universe and its social dominion, became the new historical task of the intellectual. Max Weber's *Wertfreiheit*, after Nietzsche's tragic disenchantment, is the most radical "manifesto" of the rejection of any compromise between science and ideology. *Wertfreiheit* means precisely freedom *from* value. It is value that is now seen as an impediment. The scientific statute has only one obligation, that of "self-control," which is "the only means of ensuring against deceptions, of precisely distinguishing the logicocomparative relation of reality with ideal types in the logical sense, from the evaluation of reality on the basis of ideals."[24]

It should not be overlooked that for Weber *Wertfreiheit* has a dramatic significance. The intellectual, not allowing himself value judgment, courageously accepts his own obligation to be. This acceptance is in the first place the recognition of the irrational as the negative part of the system, which, since it is inseparable from the positive, is assumed along with the latter. For

24 Quoted from M. Weber, *Il metodo delle scienze storico-sociali*, Einaudi, Turin, 1958, p. 119. See also *Il lavoro intellettuale come professione, idem*, 1966. For a generalization of Weber's criticism of ideology, see K. Loewenstein, *Beiträge zur Staatssoziologie*, Tübingen 1961 (in particular the essay "Ueber des Verhältnis von politischen Ideologien und politischen Institutionen," published earlier in *Zeitschrift für Politik*, 1955). In the works of Pareto, Max Scheler, and Weber, the criticism of ideology—expressed in different veins and with varying degrees of consciousness—signifies, not only a disenchanted adherence to the datum of reality in all its ruthless manifestations, but also that of appropriating a typically Marxist tool of disputation by turning it around on itself. The reduction of Marxism to ideology has made it possible for this type of criticism to be directed against the theoretical bases of a historical materialism, misinterpreted in more or less good faith. It is to be noted, however, that in Pareto ideology—"distorted thinking"—is only a form of action and "non-scientific thinking." Here we are still within the range of a recovery of "prejudice" recognized as such. (And indeed the ultimate recovery of the irrationality of ideology is not extraneous even to Weber.)

Weber, Keynes, Schumpeter, and Mannheim, the problem lies in the means capable of making positive and negative (capital and the working class side of work) function together, of prohibiting a separation of the two terms and realizing their complementary relationship. For all these men the dominant theme is that of a future into which the entire present is projected, of a "rational" dominion of the future, of the elimination of the *risk* it brings with it.[25]

This is why Mannheim was obliged to offer a rather mystified version of the functioning and reality of utopia.[26]

Ideologists, for Mannheim, are nothing other than a "class of cultured persons" who act as *freischwebende Intellektuelle*, as thinkers who provide but justification. Their job is solely the consolidation of existing reality.[27]

For "progressive thought," on the contrary, "every

25 See A. Negri, "La teoria capitalistica dello stato nel '29: John M. Keynes," *Contropiano*, 1968, no. 1, p. 3 ff.
26 I refer in particular to Mannheim's distinction between "progressive thought" and "conservative thought": "The greater part of the integrations with which progressive thought confronts particular facts springs from rational utopia and leads to a structural vision of the totality that is and is becoming." Ideology too can be oriented toward "objects that are extraneous to reality and transcend present existence," but nevertheless ideology "concurs in consolidating the existing order. Such an incongruous orientation becomes utopian only when it tends to break the relationships of the existing order." In fact, "in all periods of history there have been ideas that transcend the existing order, but they did not perform the function of utopias. Rather, in the measure in which they were harmoniously and organically integrated with the prevalent vision of the epoch, and did not suggest revolutionary possibilities, they constituted the most fitting ideologies of the period." K. Mannheim, "Das konservative Denken," *Archiv für Sozialwissenshaft und Sozialpolitik*, 1927. But see also *idem, Ideologie und Utopie*, 3rd ed., Frankfurt 1952, which treats fully the theory of utopia as a tendency realizable in itself, capable of breaking the confines of existing reality "to let it free to develop itself in the direction of the successive order" (*op. cit.*, p. 201). Of significance is the identification of the revolutionary moment with the ideological structure of utopia. On this, see G. Therborn, *Critica e rivoluzione. La Scuola di Francoforte*, Laterza, Bari 1972.
27 K. Mannheim, "Das konservative Denken," *cit.*

single thing receives its significance only from some other thing that is ahead of it or above it, from a *utopia of the future* or from a norm that exists above being." "Conservative thought," on the other hand, "deduced the significance of the particular from something that stands behind it, from the past or from that which already exists at least in embryonic form."[28]

Utopia is therefore nothing other than "a structural vision of the totality that is and is becoming,"[29] the transcendence of the pure "datum," a system of orientation intent upon "breaking the relationships of the existing order" in order to recover them at a higher and different level.[30] For Weber and Mannheim, the revision of ideology is one of the dynamic factors of development. For both—as for Keynes—the only readily identifiable reality is the *dynamic of development.* Mannheim's utopia, beyond its author's affirmations, is the prefiguration of final and universal models, in terms of the given reality. The "criticism of conservative thought" thus becomes a necessity, an instrument for liberating the dynamic functioning of the system. The constant rupture of equilibrium must be turned into an anti-ideological "scientific politics," into

28 *Ibid.*
29 *Ibid.*
30 It is important to note that for Mannheim, once affirmed, utopia is again transformed into ideology. Between ideology and utopia he thus establishes a dialectic relationship, which could well have given rise to reflection, even within his own treatise, on the profoundly structural character of utopia itself. It is only too clear that Mannheim's theses are an attempt at an answer to the clear understanding of the functionality of utopia contained in *German Ideology,* in the *Manifesto of the Communist Party* itself, and in Engel's *Socialism: Utopian and Scientific.* In other words, the theory of the "revolutionary change" seen as *necessary* on utopian grounds is revealed to be intimately related to social-democratic political practice, a fact easily verified by an attentive analysis of the history of the last fifty years.

a rational solution of the conflicts generated by development, but only after it has been recognized that those conflicts are inherent in reality's dialectic process.[31]

The contradiction still existing in Mannheim—utopia as a model entirely immersed in the real dynamics of politicoeconomic processes, and its character of experimental anticipation projected into the future—is a part of the whole climate of intellectual work of the avant-garde at the beginning of the twentieth century.

But with Keynes and Weber the road is already marked out: utopia must "work" within the field of programing and must abandon the field of general ideology. Mannheim expresses the awareness of a discrepancy, which still represents a danger—the only danger menacing the process of continual restructuralization of the real—between the rationality of the project, its means of implementation, and the social consciousness of the necessity of development.

But even Mannheim works within Weber's hypothesis of intellectual work that rejects any negative utopia. Seen in this light, Mannheim's criticism of ideology is consistent with the intention of rendering scientific the political control over the dynamics of the system.

It is in this way, as Cacciari has acutely observed, that the disenchantment of Weber's negation of value as a measure of judgment really takes its place as the ultimate consequence of Nietzsche's negative and "scandalous" affirmation of the subject. In Cacciari's words:

31 See K. Mannheim, "Wissenssoziologie," *Handwörterbuch der Soziologie*, Stuttgart 1931; and M. Weber, *Gesammeltepolitische Schriften*, 2nd ed., Tübingen 1958.

Weber removes this "scandal": by now the subject can only be the subject-function, precisely the intellectual, or otherwise one must go back . . . to the old illusions and deceptions of the "god who speaks to us," of the "god in me," in a word, to the substantiality of the Ego . . . To abolish all retrogressive processes is, above all, to make the Ego that which it is and must be in the irreversible context of its "destiny."[32]

If the subject is now the system, liberty from value is liberty from subjectivity itself. The relativity of value must not be the object of new "sacred sciences." The desacralization of intellectual activity is but the necessary premise for the correct functioning of that activity within the process of self-rationalization of that system.

This was also the main objective of the historical avant-garde movements. The specific aim of Futurism and Dada was just such a desacralization of values, considered to be the new, unique value. For Ball, as for Tzara, the destruction and the rendering ridiculous of

32 M. Cacciari, "Sulla genesi del pensiero negativo," *Contropiano*, 1969, no. 1, pp. 186–187. Extremely important is the connection Cacciari has established beyond doubt between Nietzsche's criticism of values and Weber's *use* of that negation. Cacciari writes: "The criticism, implicit and explicit, in all of Nietzsche, of the idea of *Vergeistigung* is intended precisely to underline the separation of the *Geist* from the general process of rationalization; or, better, to emphasize how that *Vergeistigung* is to be understood as useful to the *material life*, to the preservation *in* the process, of the capitalist system. That *Geist* is no longer *Kultur*, extraneous or even contrary to the process of the system . . . , but the rationalization of the system, of its all-embracing *existence*" (*op. cit.*, p. 182). Nietzsche's *happy science* consists in just this: in recognizing itself as an active, effective principle of an existence accepted in the entirety of its contradictions. Nietzsche's *disenchantment* is therefore the predecessor of Weber's acceptance of "destiny." For both Nietzsche and Weber "to emancipate the ideology *of the* system from the problematic question of 'values' is to find the true scientific mentality, also and precisely when they see that it is *this* system which is liberated from values and which insists on imposing itself. Therefore ideology is *true* only in the measure in which it is coherent with and structurally functional to this material process, and in the measure in which it criticizes and opposes anything putting this process in doubt or crisis" (*op. cit.*, p. 183).

the entire historic heritage of the Western bourgeoisie were conditions for the *liberation* of the potential, but inhibited, energies of that bourgeoisie itself. Or, better, of a renewed bourgeoisie, capable of accepting doubt as the premise for the full acceptance of existence as a whole, as explosive, revolutionary vitality, prepared for permanent change and the unpredictable.

The "Dadaist revolution," much more than that of the Surrealists, lies precisely in the courage to explode the contradiction which belongs to the system by placing itself before it as reality. Liberation *from* value in this sense signifies establishing the premises for action in *that* reality, in that field of indeterminant, fluid, and ambiguous forces. For this reason all interpretations of Dadaism or Futurism as hermetic self-recognitions of the irrational, or as *cupio dissolvi* in it, must be considered completely erroneous. For the avant-garde movements the destruction of values offered a wholly new type of rationality, which was capable of coming face to face with the negative, in order to make the negative itself the release valve of an unlimited potential for development. The cynicism of the avant-garde—at least where it is explicit—is nothing but the "disposition" to this ideology of development, of the revolution of individual and collective behavior, of the complete dominion over existence.

What Walter Benjamin calls the "end of the aura" expresses this exactly: the integration of the subjective moment with the complex mechanism of rationalization, but at the same time the identification of an "ethic of rationalization" completely directed upon itself. The processes of the concentration of capital, its socialization, and the constant rise of its organic composition make such an ethic necessary. This is no longer presented as an external value; it is removed from the relativity of ideological invention. The ethic of development has to be realized *together* with development, *within* development's processes. The promise of liberation from the machine can only arise from an accurately controlled image of the future.[33]

Also, there has existed no avant-garde movement whose own "political" objective was not, implicitly or explicitly, the liberation from work. This was true of the political manifesto of the Berlin Dadaists and those of Marinetti, as well as the "manifesto of luxury" of Valentine de Saint-Pont.[34] Significantly, the road to this objective indicated by the avant-garde—the case of Soviet productivism and Constructivism is a prime example — is the full affirmation of the *ideology of work*. This contradiction is permissible because the "new work" they proposed was presented as collective work, and what counts most, as planned.[35]

In the first twenty years of this century, the European avant-garde's campaign of desacralization was

33 In this sense it is not difficult to see in Marcuse's utopianism—at least in the Marcuse of *Reason and Revolution* and *Eros and Civilization*—an attempt at ethical recovery, based wholly on the negative. With a very different intellectual depth this anti-Hegelian rediscovery of the negative is found in Ernst Bloch: see E. Bloch, *Geist der Utopie*, Munich 1918, and *idem*, *Freiheit und Ordnung. Abriss der Sozialutopien*, Berlin 1947. The ethical value of utopia, as an ultimate humanistic recovery, is also at the center of Martin Buber's *Pfade in Utopia*, Heidelberg 1950 (Eng. trans. translated by R. Hull, *Paths in Utopia*, Beacon Press, Boston 1958).
34 See in particular R. Huelsenbeck, *En avant Dada: Eine Geschichte des Dadaismus*, Hannover-Leipzig-Vienna-Zurich 1920; and Valentine de Saint-Pont, *Manifesto futurista della Lussuria*, Paris, 11 January 1913.
35 On this see the fundamental essay by F. Dal Co, "Poétique de l'avant-garde et architecture dans les années '20 en Russie," *VH 101*, 1972, pp. 13-50.

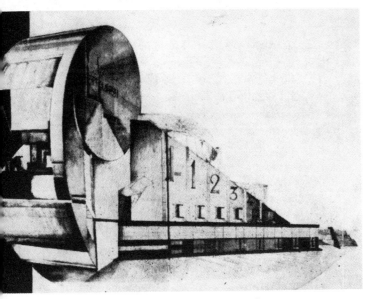

8 *Left*, Aleksandra Exter, construction for "Scene plastique et gymnastique," gouache, 1926. M. Knoedler & Co., Inc., New York. *Right*, Konstantin Mel'nikov, project for the Central Theatre of Moscow, 1931 (not realized).

carried out completely in terms of this recognition of
the new function of intellectual work. Development's
dynamic and dialectic character having been revealed, a
plan was required against the constant danger of internal deflagration. It is in this way that, demolishing
the old orders and stressing reality as the "realm of
absurdity," the avant-garde threw itself into ideological anticipations, into *partial utopias* of the plan.

By now ideology is given once and for all in the form
of a dialectic that is founded on the negative, that
makes the contradiction the propelling factor of development, that recognizes the reality of the system *starting from the presence of the contradiction.* Such a
dialectic no longer need return continually to ideology.
Not constituting an abstract scheme of behavior, but,
rather, defining at one and the same time the real bases
of the interrelationships of capitalist production and a
strategy of planning, this ideology does away with any
utopian model and any possibility of the development
of ideology itself. In other words, any reelaboration of
ideology carried out in an institutional system of values
is but pure and simple repetition. Ideology can only
pass again through the same stages already passed, continually finding the highest form of itself in the form of
the *mediation of the contradiction.* At most, "technical"
progress will be possible in the transfer of ideology to
various disciplines (but concerning this the experience
of the literary and artistic neo-avant-garde has much to
teach the contemporary high priests of disciplinary
commitment.) The real problem is to know to what extent ideology's continual repetition of itself still pre-
serves the essential roles it filled in the phase of initia-

tion and stabilization of the bourgeois-capitalist system.

Even in its most elevated form, the one made manifest in utopia, ideology is in contradiction with the developed capitalist system. It is no longer of any use to simply establish that the negative is inherent in the system. The problem posed is completely "technical," completely concerned with identifying, within the economic-productive base, the real, concrete factors which *actually make this "negativity"* (the negative of the working class) *function* as a "necessity" intrinsic to the processes of the system.[36]

No longer Hegel but Keynes, not the ineffectual ideology of plans but the plan in the concreteness of its development, not the ideology of the New Deal but post-Keynesian economy. Ideology, become concrete and stripped of any trace of utopianism, now descends directly into individual fields of endeavor; which is the same as saying that it is suppressed.

All the bourgeois talk about the "crisis of ideology" hides precisely this reality. The lament over the crisis is only an indication of an unhealthy nostalgia for the tradition based on *Kultur*'s ineffectuality.

The plan tends, on one hand, to be identified with the institution that supports it, and on the other, to be set forth as a specific institution in itself. The dominion of capital is thus realized strictly in terms of the logic of its own mechanisms, without any extrinsic justifications,

36 Typical examples of this are the theories of Abendroth and Dahrendorf on the necessary integration of competition into the factory and into society. See R. Dahrendorf, *Soziale Klassen und Klassenkonflikt in der industriellen Gesellschaft*, Stuttgart 1957; and W. Abendroth, *Antagonistische Gesellschaft und politische Demokratie*, Neuweid-Berlin 1967.

absolutely independent of any abstract "ethical" end, of any teleology, or any "obligation to be."

There did exist, however, a common element relating the intellectual anticipations of the first decades of the twentieth century to one another. What the theories of Weber, Max Scheler, or Mannheim sanctioned as a "necessary" shift of method in the structure of intellectual work, what Keynes and later Schumpeter lead back to the terms of an economic plan which presupposes a highly articulated functioning of capital in its totality, and what the ideologies of the avant-garde introduced as a proposal for social behavior, was the transformation of traditional ideology into utopia, as a prefiguration of an abstract final moment of development coincident with a global rationalization, with a *positive realization of the dialectic.*

This may appear inexact in the case of Weber or Keynes. In fact, what still remains in them of utopia is only a residue, which is completely transformed into a dynamic model once capital has resolved the problem of creating new institutions capable of making its own internal contradictions function as the propelling factors of development. Now the economic models are devised *starting from the crisis* and not abstractly, *against* it. And certainly the modern ideologies "of the contradiction" are not extraneous to such a positive realization of the dialectic.

Consequently, in the first decades of this century, there was an acceleration of the fragmentation of the functional division of intellectual work. Its position in the cycles and programing of capitalist development remains an open question, but it is certain that intellectual work which has the courage to recognize itself as capitalist science and to function accordingly is objectively separate from the backward, regressive role of purely ideological work. From now on synthesis is impossible. Utopia itself marks out the successive stages of its own extinction.

This is a separation destined to become always more extreme, as the gap widens between the institutions that realize the plan technically and those that control the dynamics of it.

In the concrete historic reality of the years following 1917 and the Treaty of Versailles, these tendencies were fully felt in the profound contradictions that shook European and American capitalism. It would be wholly antihistoric to imagine a completely operative capitalist consciousness in terms of a project directed to the creation of new institutions for a capital aware that it must be transformed into social capital, and as such manage directly its own cycles, crises, and development.

But it would also be false objectivity to underline the evident imbalances, the political backwardness, the pronouncements and internal arguments that characterize the 1920s as one blind raving, interrupted only by a few genial prophecies of a comprehensive nature.

From the point of view of our particular analysis, however, it must be emphasized that, precisely in that crushing criticism, the work of the intellectuals seems to have been directed to devising hypotheses intended for the most part to redimension cultural work itself. The real problem was one of taking sides on the question of whether or not intellectual work should be *political.* The avant-garde now presumed to set itself at the head of "social redemption."

Let us try here to compare two apparently irreconcilable points of view on this question.

In 1926, defending the absolute autonomy of literature as a "verbal art" not reducible to reasons extraneous to its construction, Victor Sklovsky wrote, "We Futurists connect our art with the Third International. But this, comrades, is a surrender to discretion! It is a Belinsky-Vengerov, it is the *Story of the Russian Intelligentsia!*"[37] Making more explicit his stand against "committed" art, against an art of agitation and propaganda advocated by Mayakovsky and the magazine *Lef,* Sklovsky continued, "I do not wish to defend art in the name of art, but, rather, propaganda in the name of propaganda . . . Agitation carried out in sung works, films, and art exhibitions is useless. It finishes by destroying itself. In the name of agitation, take it away from art!"[38]

In 1924, in the second Surrealist manifesto, André Breton recognized that thought "cannot do other than oscillate between the awareness of its perfect autonomy and that of its strict dependence." Immersed in this contradiction, given as necessary and insurmountable, Breton opted for a literature "unconditioned and conditioned, utopian and realistic, that sees its own end

37 V. Sklovsky, "Ulla, Ulla Marziani!" *Chod Konja,* Moscow-Berlin 1926. See also the analysis of the relations between the avant-garde, formalism, and political patronage contained in my essay, "Il socialismo realizzato e la crisi delle avanguardie," in the volume by various authors, *Socialismo, città, architettura. URSS 1917-1937,* 2nd ed., Officina, Rome 1972, p. 41 ff. and the bibliography cited there.
38 V. Sklovsky, *op. cit.*

only in itself and wishes nothing but to serve."

Concerning this passage of Breton, Enzensberger has commented that "the Surrealists elevated the squaring of the circle to their program."[39] That program, however, was not specifically Surrealist, but the merit of Surrealism lies historically in having made explicit the aspirations of all the avant-garde intellectuals who chose to flee from the terrain of politics, in order to safeguard a last stronghold from which to defend intellectual work in its institutional forms.

In reality the declarations of Sklovsky and Breton do not represent a reactionary ideological project that clashes with an "advanced" one. Formalism and Surrealism essentially agreed in defending the "professionality" of intellectual work. The only difference is that, the former, with greater lucidity and courage, succeeded in confessing its own tautological character, its own outdatedness (at least up to 1926), while the latter elected to set itself up as the emblem of an intellectual "bad conscience."

It is equally important to note, however, that whereas formalism—and with it the abstract avant-garde in all fields of visual and literary communication — took shape as a school for *work on the language*, Surrealism — and with it all the "committed" avant-garde — tended to present itself directly as a political intervention.

We are here faced with two tendencies, following two different and complementary directions, that were to be perpetuated up to our own day:

1 The self-recognition of intellectual work as essen-

39 H.M. Enzensberger, "Gemeinplätze, die neueste Literatur betreffend," in *Kursbuch*, 15, Frankfurt 1968.

tially *work* pure and simple, and therefore not something able to serve a revolutionary movement. The autonomy of such work is recognized explicitly as *relative*, only the political or economic patron being able to give a *sense* to the efforts of the intellectual disciplines.

2 An intellectual work that negates itself as such, claiming a position of pure ideology, and that itself wants to substitute the political organization, or to honor or criticize it from within. Its objective, however, is always to get out of productive work and stand before it as its *critical conscience*.[40]

There thus arises the problem of mediation between these two positions. This is the great theme of Benjamin, of Constructivist art and architecture, of the social-democratic techniques of administration of the city, as well as of the urban utopias of central Europe of the 1930s.

These two movements have but one ultimate significance. The intellectual avant-garde had to occupy an area from which until now it had attentively kept its distance: that of *work*. It being no longer possible to maintain the distance from productive work, which in the past had ensured the *sacredness* of intellectual research, there was nothing for the intellectual avant-garde to do but voluntarily take the plunge. This, however, implied the destruction of its own classic role. Benjamin's "end of the aura" is not induced only by the general application of new production methods, but is also the result of a conscious choice. Embedded within

40 This subject has been very lucidly treated by A. Asor Rosa in his essay "Lavoro intellettuale e utopia dell'avanguardia nel paese del socialismo realizzato," in *Socialismo, città, architettura, cit.*, p. 217 ff.

the choice is all the will to survive contained in the fierce anti-institutional battle undertaken by "negative thought."

Also not to be overlooked is the plea made to the intellectuals by the most advanced areas of capital in the twenties and thirties. Rathenau and Ford made their pleas very explicit. Henry Ford stated:

We want artists in industrial relationship. We want masters in industrial method — both from the standpoint of the producer and the product. We want those who can mould the political, social, industrial, and moral mass into a sound and shapely whole. We have limited the creative faculty too much and have used it for too trivial ends. We want men who can create the working design for all that is right and good and desirable in our life.[41]

Ford does not presume that the intellectual enter directly into control of the production cycle, but he does presume that the intellectual's contribution clearly and explicitly "attributes sense" to that cycle. By entering the sphere of work, ideological production is simultaneously attracted and repelled. On the one hand, it is asked to produce global models. In this task the work of pure reason must not be divorced from social ends: the innovating models must correspond simultaneously to the needs of given moments, both for the restructuring of the production cycle and for the distribution of merchandise. On the other hand, ideology must have a direct effect on the socialization of consumption. Having entered the sphere of productive work—but itself not yet transformed into productive

41 H. Ford, *My Life and Work*, Doubleday, Page & Co., Garden City, N.Y., 1923, p. 104.

work—intellectual endeavor is driven to make ideological production more functional.

Significant in this respect is the correspondence between the proposals of the German left-wing intellectuals after World War I and Walter Rathenau's *Die neue Wirtschaft*. In 1918 Rathenau wrote:

The order we will reach will be a system, like the present one, of private economy, but not a private economy without controls. It will have to be imbued with a collective will, that same will which today imbues any jointly responsible human work.[42]

Thus were laid the foundations of "democratic capitalism," with notable theoretical consequences in the field of economy and in the organization of the city. Rathenau, in fact, continued:

The new prosperity of the cities will have to have its foundation in the city soil itself, which has not grown for either the builders who earn millions or those who have cornered the market on building ground, construction speculators, and rent tyrants . . . On the contrary, in a few generations the city soil on which the new constructions face will have to become the free property of the municipalities. As long as the architectural negligence of our streets exists, it will be a testimony and admonition of the negligence of our economic concepts. These concepts have granted to a monopolistic caste a right of taxation, arbitrarily augmentable by them, on the common heritage, and have made a gift of millions upon millions to the holders of urban property investments.[43]

Such antimonopolistic intonations in Rathenau

42 W. Rathenau, *Die neue Wirtschaft*, Berlin 1918.
43 *Ibid.*

should not come as a surprise. Regarding this phenomenon, Cacciari has acutely observed:

The capitalist counterattack assumes for itself and
redefines the fundamental elements of "socialist"
strategy. Socialism as accelerated accumulation, industrial reconstruction, and state intervention in the
economic cycle, *but above all* as a *universal defense* of
live work . . . The *Sozialismus* of large German capital,
between 1918 and 1921, thus guarantees itself an
organic relationship in actual fact with the political and
trade-union organization of the working class. And it is
inevitable that this phase be obdurately swept away
when, after any danger of an autonomous organization
at the working-class level has been destroyed, capital
can again assume *directly* the *social* management and
organization of its own cycle.[44]

Organization and planning are thus the passwords of
both democratic socialism and democratic capitalism.
Rathenau and Naumann are its spokesmen. And indeed
we should not forget Naumann's decisive role in the
formation of the ideology of the *Deutscher Werkbund*
between 1907 and 1918.[45] It was from this particular
perspective that Rathenau prognosticated a planned
and completely collective city, free of speculation.
Productive capital clearly felt the need to separate from
unproductive and parasitic capital, and this need expressed by Rathenau coincided with those advanced by
the urban planners.

44 M. Cacciari, *Sul problema dell'organizzazione, cit.,* p. 11.
45 See F. Naumann, *Werkbund und Weltwirtshaft,* Werkbund-Ausstellung,
Cologne 1914, found also in J. Posener, *Anfänge des Funktionalismus. Von
Arts and Crafts zum deutschen Werkbund,* Ullstein Bauwelt Fundamente,
Berlin-Frankfurt 1964, pp. 223-225; H. Eckstein, "Idee und Geschichte des
deutschen Werkbundes, 1907–1957," and T. Heuss, "Notizen und Excurse zur
Geschichte des deutschen Werkbundes," both in *50 Jahre Deutscher Werk-
bund,* Alfred Metzner Verlag, Berlin-Frankfurt 1958.

Further on I shall speak of the social-democratic administration of German cities between 1923 and 1933. Here I only point out that Rathenau's insistence on programing and freedom from speculation was part of a tradition that had its origin in the nineteenth century, in Huber's attempts at a cooperative solution for workmen's housing in Berlin, a tradition that after 1924 was to give rise to the avant-garde administration of Frankfurt under the guidance of Burgomaster Landmann.

This anti-institutional phase of the avant-garde intelligentsia is thus seen to have been of use in the criticism of outworn values. All the work of demolition served to prepare a clean-swept platform from which to depart in discovery of the new "historic tasks" of intellectual work.

It should also be born in mind that these historic tasks carried on a dialogue with two different interlocutors simultaneously. In the first place there was the mystic colloquy with capital, understood as abstract technology, or as the universal productive subject. In the second place, there was the mystic colloquy with the masses, understood as an equally abstract subject, endowed with an ethical significance (the O'Mench of Expressionism and Linkskommunismus). Ideology assumed for itself the task of unifying the subject and the object of production. In other words, ideology was transformed into *capitalistic-industrial utopia*. And this is true whether it took the form of ideology completely involved with the work process, or ideology as an abstract project of the socialization of work. At this point we must stress that the analysis made here touches only marginally the capitalist viewpoint. The

9 Grosvenor Atterbury, architect, and Frederick Law Olmsted, Jr.,
planner, the town center of Forest Hill Garden, Queens, New York,
1910–1913. This first "romantic suburb" of New York was spon-
sored by the Russell Sage Foundation. Photo by M. Tafuri.

convergence of ideas of the intellectual avant-garde and advanced capital, emphasized above, is not indicative of a general phenomenon. Rather, that very convergence is seen historically to be quite limited and temporary, and operative in but marginal sectors of development. It is therefore important to understand both the subjective character of the choice made by intellectual work, and the constant marginalization it underwent within capitalist development. Utopia became of service to development as a reserve of tendentious models and as an arm for the extraction of consensus.

It is clear that these functions of utopia were to be in crisis each time the objectives of the tendentious models were required to prove themselves in reality, and each time that manipulation of consensus showed itself to be unsuited to the aims of development.

Instead of really choosing between the aspiration to absolute autonomy or voluntary self-effacement in a mission of "class service," ideology ended, in most cases and with a surprising consistency of behavior, by precariously straddling the borderline between these two choices.

The aspiration to the autonomy of intellectual endeavor was a continuation of the project for recovering the subjectivity expropriated by the capitalist division of work. Intellectual work as "class service" was a project for restoring—indirectly—that same subjectivity to the class from which it had been expropriated. It seems hardly necessary to underline the "poverty" of these two ideological directions; I am here only exposing the complementary character of their objectives. Literature and art as means of recovering Totality and of transfering it to the new historic subject by election—the working class—were part of a design that took its place in the rear guard of capitalist development. And this is true even if that design fulfilled precise duties in that development.

What is of greater interest is the way in which these two choices (or the compromise mediating them) were realized.

Among all the historical avant-garde movements, autonomy of formal construction no longer necessarily meant controlling daily experience through form. They were now disposed to accept the idea that it is experience that dominates the subject. The problem was *to plan the disappearance of the subject,* to cancel the anguish caused by the pathetic (or ridiculous) resistance of the individual to the structures of domination that close in upon him, to indicate the voluntary and docile submission to those structures of domination that close in upon him, to indicate the voluntary and docile submission to those structures of domination as the promised land of universal planning: paradise on earth is realized through the "disappearance of the tragic."[46]

46 Extremely interesting are the reactions to the awareness of this *dissolution of tragedy,* in the 1920s and 30s, on the part of the advanced theorists of the capitalist bourgeoisie and on the part of "left-wing communism." For the latter, the intellectual opposition to the capitalist destruction of the bourgeois *Geist,* of the utopia of Form, of "problematic" humanism, was identified with the tendency to recover such castoff ideological instruments by delivering them into the hands of the proletariat. *Marxist humanism* is thus seen as a project for the extension to the working class of the "Form-Utopia of the bourgeoisie which is Tragedy": the bourgeois hero is transformed into the *collective hero.* Such a process is very clear in the thought of the young Lukács, as in Lukács the Marxist, but also in certain passages of Korsch and Löwith, and—as pure ideology—in Bertolt Brecht. See A. Asor Rosa, "Il giovane Lukács teorico dell'arte borghese," *Contropiano,* 1968, no. 1, p. 59 ff.; and G. Bedeschi, *Alienazione e feticismo nel pensiero di Marx,* 2nd ed., Laterza, Bari 1972 (in particular, app. I, p. 117 ff.).

Salvation lies no longer in "revolt," but in surrender without discretion. Only a humanity that has absorbed and made its own the ideology of work, that does not persist in considering production and organization *something other* than itself or simply instruments, that *recognizes itself to be part of a comprehensive plan* and as such fully accepts that it must *function* as the cogwheels of a global machine: only this humanity can atone for its "original sin." And this sin is not in having created a system of means without knowing how to control the "revolt of the objects" against their inventor, as Löwith and the young Lukács understood Marxist alienation. This sin consists instead in *man's "diabolical" insistence on remaining man*, in taking his place as an "imperfect machine" in a social universe in which the only consistent behavior is that of pure silence.[47]

This was exactly the ideology that informed the Futurist manifestos, Dadaist mechanicalism, *De Stijl*

47 "General proletarianization thus remains the last great substratum of the unitary appearance of the human condition: a cursed irony of capitalist society, the condemnation to an irremediable distance from *real* proletarianization precisely at the moment when a *formal* proletarianization is taking place. Just when the whole society seems modeled on the factory, when identical form seems to have been achieved and circulates throughout the system, it is discovered that this appearance is repugnant to thought, which must always seek beyond itself a margin of diversity and live *for* that diversity. It is even ready to sacrifice itself for that, to consider itself circulating merchandise, or a pure function in the general circulation of merchandise. On the one hand, a synthetic form (become a reality for the first time in history), which is the general exploitation of the working class; on the other, no form, only a piece of circulating capital." (N. Licciardello, "Proletarizzazione e utopia," *Contropiano*, 1968, no. 1, p. 109). Here we can only briefly refer to the function of the artistic avant-garde movements of the twentieth century, and the theoretical thought accompanying them, in making concrete and visible the *formal proletarianization* of which Licciardello speaks. The utopia of the avant-garde consists precisely in the planned recovery of a "unitary appearance of the human condition," ensured by intellectual work which saves itself by destroying its own foundation.

10 Francis Picabia, *Mechanical Composition*, 1919. Mr. and Mrs.
Lester Arnet Collection, New York.

elementarism, and international Constructivism. But what is really striking in this ideology of unconditional consensus is its ingenuous radicalism. Among all those literary, artistic, or cinematographic manifestos in favor of the *mechanization of the universe*, there is not one that does not fail to amaze when compared with the ends it seems to propose. These invitations to become a machine, to universal proletarianization, to forced production, in revealing the ideology of the Plan all too explicitly, cannot fail to arouse suspicion as to their real intentions.

"Negative thought" had enunciated its own project for survival in its refutation of the Hegelian dialectic and a recovery of the contradictions this had eliminated. "Positive thought" does nothing but overturn that negativeness on itself. The negative is revealed as such, even in its "ineluctability." Resignation to it is only a first condition for making possible the perpetuation of the intellectual disciplines; for making possible the recovery for intellectual work (at the price of destroying its "aura") of the tradition of its "sacred" extraneousness to the world; for providing a reason, no matter how minimal, for its survival. The downfall of reason is now acclaimed the realization of reason's own historic mission. In its cynicism intellectual work plays its cards to the ambiguous limit of irony.

The demonstration beyond question that there is no other way but to nullify the human subject in the subject of development, is a task tending to preserve ideology as an ultimate cultural *project*. The "freedom from value," the separation of *Geist* from the general process of rationalization, and the neutralization of any project

of ethical justification of the logic of the system, have
already taken place. They must now impose themselves with the force of a datum. They can, at least,
demonstrate their efficiency. This is why any residue of
value must be violently desecrated. The fight against
man is conditioned by the needs of development, and
only if development encounters obstacles—due to the
persistence of traditional prejudices—will it be possible
to repropose a human mythology. This will, of course,
be a cynical and regressive mythology, serving to break
down only weak resistance.[48]

48 This can be felt in the pessimism of Lévi-Strauss, completely dominated by
an absolute of the *human*, that by not corresponding with reality produces the
structuralist outlook of a *reconstructing-for-nothing*, of an *exit from the world*,
provoked by the "betrayal" of the world itself. ". . . for what is the use of action,
if the thinking which guides that action leads to the discovery of meaningless-
ness? . . . The world began without the human race and it will end without it.
The institutions, manners, and customs which I shall have spent my life in
cataloguing and trying to understand are an ephemeral efflorescence of a
creative process in relation to which they are meaningless . . . As for the
creations of the human mind, they are meaningful only in relation to that mind
and will fall into nothingness as soon as it ceases to exist." C. Lévi-Strauss,
Tristes tropiques, Plon, Paris 1955. Eng. trans., *A World on the Wane*,
translated by J. Russell, Criterion Books, New York, n.d. Translation first
published under the title, *Tristes Tropiques*, *idem*, 1961, pp. 410, 414.

4 The Dialectic of the Avant-Garde

The "downfall of reason" was felt persistently in one specific area: that of the metropolis. It is not merely coincidence that the subject of the *Grossstadt* dominates the thought of Simmel, Weber, and Benjamin, with obvious influence on architects and theorists such as August Endell, Karl Scheffler, and Ludwig Hilberseimer.[49]

The "loss" foretold by Piranesi has now become tragic reality. The experience of the "tragic" is the experience of the metropolis.

In face of such an inevitable experience, the intellectual is no longer even able to assume the *blasé* attitude of a Baudelaire.

As Ladislao Mittner has effectively written concerning Döblin, the "mysticism of passive resistance" characterizes the Expressionist protest: "he who reacts loses the world, he who wants to cling to it loses it just the same."[50]

It is important to note that in criticizing Engels' "moral reaction" to the city crowd, Benjamin uses

49 I refer here to the volumes by A. Endell, *Die Schönheit der Grossstadt*, Strecher und Schröder, Stuttgart 1908; K. Scheffler, *Die Architektur der Grosstadt*, Bruno Cassier, Berlin 1913; and L. Hilberseimer, *Grosstadtarchitektur*, Julius Hoffmann Verlag, Stuttgart 1927.
50 A. Döblin, *Die drei Sprünge des Wang-Lun*, 1915. See L. Mittner, *L'espressionismo*, Laterza, Bari 1965, p. 96.

Engels' own observations to introduce the subject of the general extension of working-class conditions in the urban structure. Benjamin writes:

In Engels the crowd has something alarming about it. It arouses a moral reaction in him. To this is added an aesthetic reaction: the rhythm in which the passersby encounter and pass each other is unpleasant to him. The fascination of his description lies precisely in the way his incorruptible critical nature is fused with a patriarchal tone. The author comes from a still-provincial Germany and perhaps the temptation to lose himself in a flood of human beings never crossed his mind.[51]

One may disagree with the partiality of Benjamin's reading of *The Situation of the Working Class in England*. What interests us, however, is the way in which he passes from Engels' description of the mass, of the crowd of the metropolis, to considerations of Baudelaire's relations with the mass itself. Considering Engels' and Hegel's reactions to be residues of an attitude of detachment from the new urban reality in its new qualitative and quantitative aspects, Benjamin notes that the facility and ease with which the Parisian *flâneur* moves in the crowd has become the natural behavior of the modern user of the metropolis.

No matter how great the distance he pretended to assume in respect to the crowd, [Baudelaire] was

51 W. Benjamin, *Schriften*, Suhrkamp Verlag, Frankfurt 1955. On Benjamin's role in establishing the theories of "technological art" as ideology of integration, see the recent fundamental volume by G. Pasqualotto, *Avanguardia e technologia. Walter Benjamin, Max Bense e i problemi dell'estetica technologica*, Officina, Rome 1971. This work definitively destroys the interpretations that have accumulated on Benjamin's thought, exemplified by Perlini's studies (see T. Perlini, "Dall'Utopia alla teorica critica e critica del progresso," *Communità*, 1969, nos. 159/160 and 165) and by the articles published in the magazine *Alternative* (Berlin 1968, no. 59/60).

thoroughly impregnated with it, and could not, like Engels, consider it from without. The mass is so intrinsic to Baudelaire that in his writings one looks in vain for a description of it . . . Baudelaire does not describe the population or the city. And it was precisely in avoiding this that he was able to evoke the one in the image of the other. His crowd is always that of the metropolis; his Paris is always overpopulated. This is what makes him so superior to Barbier, in whom—the procedure being description—the masses and the city are independent one from the other. In the *Tableaux parisiens*, one can almost always feel the secret presence of a mass.[52]

The presence, or rather immanence, of the real relationships of production in the behavior of the "public" who use the city, who are at the same time unconscious of being used by it, is similar to the presence of an observer such as Baudelaire. The observer-poet is forced to recognize his own unendurable position of participant in an always more general commercialization, in the very moment in which he discovers that the only inevitable necessity for the poet is by now his own prostitution.[53]

The poetry of Baudelaire, like the products shown at the universal expositions, or like the transformation of the urban morphology set in motion by Hausmann, marks the new-found awareness of the indissoluble, dynamic interconnectedness existing between uniformity and diversity. Especially for the structure of the new bourgeois city, one can still not speak of tension between the exception and the rule, but one can speak

52 W. Benjamin, *op. cit.*
53 "With the rise of the metropolis, prostitution acquires new mysteries. One of these is above all the labyrinthic character of the city itself: the image of the labyrinth has entered the blood of the *flâneur*. One might say that prostitution gives it a different color" (*ibid.*).

of tension between the obligatory commercialization of the object and the subjective attempts to recover—falsely—its authenticity.

Now, however, there is no longer any way except to reduce the search for authenticity to the search for the eccentric. It is not only the poet who has to accept his condition of mime, but rather the entire city. Objectively structured like a machine for the extraction of surplus value, in its own conditioning mechanisms the city reproduces the reality of the ways of industrial production.

Benjamin closely relates the decline of *skill* and *practice* in industrial work—still operative in handwork—to the experience of shock typical of the urban condition.

The nonspecialized worker is the one most severely degraded by the apprenticeship of the machine. His work is impervious to experience. Skill no longer has any place there. What the amusement park realizes in its flying cages and other similar diversions is only a taste of the apprenticeship to which the nonspecialized worker is subjected in the factory. . . Poe's text [Benjamin here refers to *The Man of the Crowd*, translated by Baudelaire] makes evident the relationship between unrestrained behavior and discipline. His passersby behave as if, become like automatons, they can no longer express themselves except automatically. Their behavior is a reaction to shock. "If jostled, they bowed profusely to the jostlers. . ."[54]

Between the code of behavior connected with the experience of shock and a gambling game there thus exists a strong affinity:

Each intervention on a machine is just as hermetically separated from the one that preceded it, as is a *coup* in

54 *Ibid.*

11 Botanischer Garten, Berlin. Photo by Gianni Longo.

gambling from the immediately preceding *coup*. And in a certain way the slavery of the salaried worker is pendent to that of the gambler. The work of the one and the other is equally devoid of any content.[55]

Despite the acuteness of Benjamin's observations, neither in his essays on Baudelaire, nor in "Das Kunstwerk im Zeitalter seiner technischen Reproduzierbarkeit" ("The Work of Art in the Era of Its Technical Reproducibility"), does he relate this invasion of the ways of production in the urban morphology to the response of the avant-garde movements to the subject of the city.

The arcades and department stores of Paris, like the great expositions, were certainly the places in which the crowd, itself become a spectacle, found the spatial and visual means for a self-education from the point of view of capital.[56] But throughout the nineteenth century this recreational-pedagogical experience, precisely in being concentrated in exceptional architectural types, still dangerously revealed its restricted scope. The ideology of the public is not, in fact, an end in itself. It is only a moment of the ideology of the city as a productive unity in the proper sense of the term and, simultaneously, as an instrument of coordination of the production-distribution-consumption cycle.

This is why the ideology of consumption, far from constituting an isolated or successive moment of the organization of production, must be offered to the

---

55 *Ibid.*
56 The relation between the rise of the *ideology of the public* and the program of the great expositions has been analyzed by A. Abruzzese in the essay "Spettacolo e alienazione," *Contropiano*, 1968, no. 2, pp. 379-421. On arcades see the recent and very well documented volume by J. F. Geist, *Passagen, ein Bautyp des 19. Jahrhunderts*, Bastei Verlag, Munich 1969.

public as the ideology of the correct use of the city. (It may be appropriate to recall here how much the problem of behavior influenced the experience of the European avant-garde, and the symptomatic example of Loos, who in 1903, upon his return from the United States, published two numbers of *Das Andere*, dedicated with a polemical and ironic tone to introducing into bourgeois Vienna the "modern" ways of the city-dweller.)

When the experience of the crowd became—as in Baudelaire—an endured consciousness of participation, it served to make general an operative reality, but did not contribute to its advancement. It was instead at this point, and only at this point, that the linguistic revolution of contemporary art was called upon to offer its contribution.

Free the experience of shock from any automatism; found, on the basis of that experience, visual codes and codes of action transformed by the already consolidated characteristics of the capitalist metropolis (rapidity of transformation, organization and simultaneousness of communications, accelerated tempo of use, eclecticism); reduce the artistic experience to a pure object (obvious metaphor for object-merchandise); involve the public, unified in an avowed interclass and therefore anti-bourgeois ideology: these are the tasks that all together were assumed by the avant-garde of the twentieth century.

And I must repeat, all together, and without any distinction between Constructivism and the art of protest. Cubism, Futurism, Dada, all the historical avant-garde movements arose and succeeded each other according

12 E. R. Graham (of D. Burnham & Co.), Equitable Life Insurance
Building, New York, 1913–1915.

to the typical law of industrial production, the essence of which is the continual technical revolution. For all the avant-garde movements—and not only in the field of painting—the law of assemblage was fundamental. And since the assembled objects belonged to the real world, the picture became a neutral field on which to project the *experience of the shock* suffered in the city. The problem now was that of teaching that one is not to "suffer" that shock, but to absorb it as an inevitable condition of existence.

A passage from Georg Simmel is very illuminating in this regard. Examining the characteristics of what he called "the metropolitan man," Simmel analyzed the new behavior assumed by the individual-mass within the metropolis, identified as the seat of the "money economy." The "intensification of nervous stimulation" induced by the "rapid crowding of changing images, the sharp discontinuity in the grasp of a single glance, and the unexpectedness of onrushing impressions," were interpreted by Simmel as the new conditions that generate the *blasé* attitude of the individual of the metropolis: of the "man without quality," by definition indifferent to value. Simmel observed:

The essence of the *blasé* attitude consists of the blunting of discrimination. This does not mean that the objects are not perceived, as is the case with the half-wit, but rather, that the meaning and differing values of things, and thereby the things themselves, are experienced as insubstantial. They appear to the *blasé* person in an evenly flat and grey tone; no one object deserves preference over any other. This mood is the faithful subjective reflection of a completely internalized money economy. . . *All things float with equal specific gravity in the constantly moving stream of*

13 Ernst Ludwig Kirchner, *Women in the Potsdammerplatz*, etching,
1914–1915. Civic Art Institute, Frankfurt a. M.

*money. All things lie on the same level and differ from
one another only in the size of the area which they
cover.*[57]

Massimo Cacciari has penetratingly analyzed the
specific sense of Simmel's sociology.[58] For us now it is
of interest to note that Simmel's considerations on the
great metropolis, written between 1900 and 1903, contained *in nuce* the problems that were to be at the center
of concern of the historical avant-garde movements.
The objects all floating on the same plane, with the
same specific gravity, in the constant movement of the
money economy: does it not seem that we are reading
here a literary comment on a Schwitter *Merzbild*? (It
should not be forgotten that the very word *Merz* is but
a part of the word *Commerz*.) The problem was, in fact,
how to render active the intensification of nervous

57 G. Simmel, *Die Grossstädt und das Geistesleben*, Dresden 1903 (Eng. trans.,
"The Metropolis and Mental Life," in *The Sociology of Georg Simmel*,
translated and edited by Kurt H. Wolff, Free Press, New York 1950, pp. 409-
424). Emphasis supplied.

58 M. Cacciari, "Note sulla dialettica del negativo nell'epoca della metropoli
(Saggio su Georg Simmel)," in *Angelus Novus*, 1971, no. 21, p. 1 ff. Cacciari
writes: "The process of *internalization* of the money economy marks the con-
clusive and fundamental point of Simmel's analysis. It is at this point that the
realization of the dialectic process takes place concretely and the preceding
determinants cease to count 'in general'. When the *intellectualized* multiplicity
of the stimuli becomes *behavior*, then and only then the *Vergeistigung* is complete, then and only then is it certain that no individual autonomy exists outside
of it. And in order that the proof of this be completely valid, the domination of
the form, derived from the abstraction and calculation native to the metropolis,
must be demonstrated in the most apparently 'eccentric' behavior . . . The *blasé*
attitude defines the *illusiveness of the differences*. Its constant nervous stimulation and the search for pleasure prove to be experiences completely abstract
from the specific individuality of their object: 'no object deserves preference
over any other' " (Simmel, *loc. cit.*) Cacciari continues: "Intellectualization,
Vergeistigung, and commercialization are all brought together in the *blasé* attitude: with it the metropolis finally creates its 'type', its structure 'in general'
finally becomes a social reality and a cultural fact. It is money that has here
found its most authentic bearer." See, also by Cacciari: *Metropolis. Saggi sulla
grande città di Sombart, Endell, Scheffler, Simmel*, Officina, Rome 1973, as
well as his introductory essay to G. Simmel, *Saggi di estetica*, Livinia, Padua
1970.

stimulation (*Nervenleben*); how to absorb the shock provoked by the metropolis by transforming it into a new principle of dynamic development; how to "utilize" to the limit the anguish which "indifference to value" continually provokes and nourishes in the metropolitan experience. It was necessary to pass from Munch's *Scream* to El Lissitzky's *Story of Two Squares*: from the anguished discovery of the nullification of values, to the use of a language of pure signs, perceptible by a mass that had completely absorbed the universe without quality of the money economy.

The laws of production thus became part of a new universe of conventions, explicitly put forth as "natural." This is the reason why the avant-garde movements did not concern themselves with the problem of a *rapproachment* with the public. On the contrary, this was a problem that could not even be posed. Doing nothing other than interpreting something necessary and universal, the avant-garde could accept temporary unpopularity, well knowing that their break with the past was the fundamental condition for their value as models for action.

Art as a model of action. This was the great guiding principle of the artistic redemption of the modern bourgeoisie. But it was at the same time an absolute which gave rise to new and irrepressible contradictions. Life and art having been revealed antithetical, there had to be found, either means of mediation—following this road the entire artistic production accepted the problematic as its new ethical horizon—or ways by which art could pass into life, even if the Hegelian prophecy of the *death of art* thus became a reality.

It is here that the relationships bringing together the great tradition of bourgeois art in a single whole are most concretely exposed. The illumination offered by our initial reference to Piranesi as both theoretician and critic of an art *no longer universalizing and not yet bourgeois* can now be fully appreciated. Criticism, problematicality, and the drama of utopia: these were the basic elements forming the tradition of the "modern movement." And inasmuch as it was a project for modelling the "bourgeois man" as an absolute type, the "modern movement" had its own undeniable, internal coherence (even if this is not the coherence recognized in it by current historical study).

Both Piranesi's *Campo Marzio* and Picasso's *Dame au violon* are "projects," though the former organizes an architectural dimension and the latter a human mode of behavior. Both use the technique of shock, even if Piranesi's etching adopts preformed historical material and Picasso's painting artificial material (just as later Duchamp, Hausmann and Schwitter were to do even more pointedly). Both discover the reality of a machine-universe: even if the eighteenth century urban project renders that universe as an abstraction and reacts to the discovery with terror, and the Picasso painting is conceived completely within this reality.

But more importantly, both Piranesi and Picasso, by means of the excess of truth acquired through their intensely critical formal elaborations, make "universal" a reality which could otherwise be considered completely particular. The "project" inherent in the Cubist painting, however, goes beyond the painting itself. Ready-made objects, introduced in 1912 by Braque and Picasso and codified as new means of communication by Duchamp, sanctioned the self-sufficiency of reality and the definitive rejection, by reality itself, of any representation. The painter could only analyze this reality. His asserted dominion over form was but a cover for something he could still not accept: that is, that by now it was form which dominated the painter.

Except that now form had to be understood as the logic of subjective reactions to the objective universe of production. Cubism as a whole tended to define the laws of such reactions. It is symptomatic that Cubism began from the subjective and ended in the most absolute rejection of it (as was to be noticed by Apollinaire with uneasiness). What Cubism as a "project" wanted to realize was a mode of behavior. Its antinaturalism, however, contained no persuasive element for the public. Instead, the intention of Cubism was to demonstrate the reality of the "new nature" created by the new capitalist metropolis and its necessary and universal character, in which necessity and liberty coincide.

For this reason Braque and Picasso, and still more Gris, adopted the technique of assemblage, which gave absolute form to the universe of the *civilization machiniste*. Primitivism and antihistoricism were the consequences and not the causes of their fundamental choices.

As techniques of analysis of a totalizing universe, both Cubism and *De Stijl* were explicit invitations to action. For their artistic products one could well speak of *the fetishization of the artistic object and its mystery*.

The public had to be provoked. Only in this way could it be actively introduced into the universe of *precision* dominated by the laws of production. The passivity of the *flâneur* sung by Baudelaire had to be conquered. The *blasé* attitude had to be transformed into effective participation in the urban scene. The city was the object to which neither Cubist painting, nor the Futurist "cuffings," nor Dadaist nihilism refer specifically, but which—precisely because continually presupposed—was the benchmark of the avant-garde movements. Mondrian was to have the courage to "name" the city as the final object toward which neoplastic composition tended. But he was to be forced to recognize that, once it had been translated into urban structures, painting—by now reduced to a pure model of behavior—would have to die.[59]

Baudelaire had discovered that the commercialization of the poetic product can be accentuated by the poet's very attempt to free himself from his objective conditions. The prostitution of the artist immediately follows his moment of maximum human sincerity.[60] *De Stijl*, and still more Dada, discovered that there are two roads to the suicide of art: silent immersion in the structure of the city by the idealization of its contradictions, or violent insertion into the structures of artistic communication of the irrational—this, too, idealized—as transformed by the city.

De Stijl became a method of formal control of the technological universe. Dada wanted to enunciate apocalyptically its immanent absurdity. And yet the

59 See P. Mondrian, *De Stijl*, I and III. See also the essay by Mondrian, "L'homme, la rue, la ville", *Vouloir*, 1927, no. 25.
60 This is very evident in Hugo Ball's attitude: see H. Ball, *Die Flucht aus der Zeit*, Lucern 1946. On Ball see the recent monograph by L. Valeriani, *Ball e il Cabaret Voltaire*, Martano, Turin 1971.

nihilist criticism formulated by Dada ended by becoming a means of control for planning. As we shall see, there is nothing surprising in encountering many points of tangency between the most "constructive" and the most destructive avant-garde movements of the Twentieth century.

Dada's ferocious decomposition of the linguistic material and its opposition to prefiguration: what were these, after all, if not the sublimation of automatism and commercialization of "values" now spread through all levels of existence by the advance of capitalism? *De Stijl* and the Bauhaus introduced the *ideology of the plan* into a design method that was always closely related to the city as a productive structure. Dada, by means of the absurd, demonstrated—without naming it—the necessity of a plan.

Furthermore, all the avant-garde movements adopted political parties as models of action. Dada and Surrealism can surely be seen as particular expressions of the anarchic spirit. And indeed *De Stijl*, the Bauhaus, and the Soviet avant-garde movements did not hesitate to set themselves up explicitly as global alternatives to political practices; alternatives that assumed all the characteristics of ethical choices.

De Stijl—and for that matter Russian Futurism and the Constructivist currents—opposed Chaos, the empirical, and the commonplace, with the principle of Form. And it was a form which took account of that which concretely impoverishes reality, rendering it formless and chaotic. The panorama of industrial production, which spiritually impoverishes the world, was dismissed as a universe "without quality," as nonvalue.

14 Kurt Schwitters, view of the *Merzbau* in Hanover, 1920–1936 (destroyed).

But it was taken up again after being transformed into new value through its sublimation. The *De Stijl* technique of the decomposition of complex into elementary forms corresponded to the discovery that the "new richness" of spirit could not be sought outside the "new poverty" assumed by mechanical civilization. The disarticulated recomposition of those elementary forms exalted the mechanical universe by demonstrating that no form can be given to the recovery of totality (of being, as of art) except form derived from the problematic nature of form itself.

Dada instead plunged into chaos. By representing chaos, it confirmed its reality; by treating it with irony, it exposed a necessity that had been lacking. This unprovided necessity was precisely that control of formlessness and chaos that *De Stijl*, all the European Constructivist currents, and even the formalist aesthetic of the nineteenth century—from *Sichtbarkeit* on—posed as the new frontier of visual communications. Thus it is not surprising that Dadaist anarchy and *De Stijl* order converged and mingled from 1922 on, from the aspect of theory as well as that of practice, in which the main concern was that of working out the means of a new synthesis.[61]

61 Indeed the subject of the unification of the contributions of the avant-garde movements appears to have been an urgent one, at least from 1922 on. In this the efforts of such figures as El Lissitzky, Moholy-Nagy, Van Doesburg, and Hans Richter were prominent. A first synthesis of Dada and Constructivism took place with the manifesto of Raoul Hausmann, Hans Arp, Ivan Puni (Jean Pougny), and László Moholy-Nagy, "Aufruf zur Elementaren Kunst," *De Stijl*, IV, 1921, no. 10, p. 156. Fundamental were the two conventions of the avant-garde held in Düsseldorf and Weimar in 1922: see *De Stijl*, V, 1922, no. 4, for the concluding manifesto of the Düsseldorf convention (May 30, 1922); and T. Van Doesburg, H. Richter, K. Maes, Max Burchartz, and El Lissitzky, "Konstruktivistische internationale schöpferische Arbeitsgemeinschaft," *De Stijl*, V, 1922, no. 8, pp. 113-115. The magazines *Mécano*, *G*, and *Merz* resulted from this synthesis.

Chaos and order were thus sanctioned by the historical avant-garde movements as the "values," in the proper sense of the term, of the new capitalist city.

Of course, chaos is a datum and order an objective. But from now on form is not sought outside of chaos; it is sought within it. It is order that confers significance upon chaos and transforms it into value, into "liberty." Even Dadaist destructiveness has a "positive" aim —particularly in America and Berlin. Indeed, historically speaking, Dadaist nihilism, in the hands of a Hausmann or a Heartfield, became the expression of a new technique of communication. The systematic use of the unexpected and the technique of assemblage were brought together to form the premises of a new nonverbal language, based on improbability and what Russian formalism called "semantic distortion." It was therefore precisely with Dadaism that the theory of information became an instrument of visual communications.

But the real place of the improbable is the city. The formlessness and chaos of the city is therefore to be redeemed by extracting from within it all its progressive virtues. The necessity of a programed control of the new forces released by technology was very clearly pointed out by the avant-garde movements, who immediately after discovered they were not capable of giving concrete form to this entreaty of Reason.

It was at this point that architecture could enter the scene, absorbing and going beyond all the entreaties of the avant-garde movements. And architecture alone being in a position to really respond to the needs indicated by Cubism, Futurism, Dada, *De Stijl*, and international

15 Georg Grosz, *Friedrichstrasse*, lithograph, 1918.

Constructivism, these movements were thrown into crisis.

The Bauhaus, as the decantation chamber of the avant-garde, fulfilled the historic task of selecting from all the contributions of the avant-garde by testing them in terms of the needs of productive reality.[62] Industrial design, a method of organizing production even before it is a method of configuring objects, did away with the residue of utopia inherent in the artistic expression of the avant-garde. Ideology now was not superimposed on artistic operations—the latter were now concrete because they were connected to the real production cycle—but had become an internal part of the operations themselves.

Despite its realism, however, even industrial design left certain needs unsatisfied; and in the impetus it gave to the organization of individual enterprises and the organization of production it contained a margin of utopia. But this was now a utopia serving the objectives of the reorganization of production. The plan common to the spearhead architectural movements—the term avant-garde is here no longer adequate—from the for-

62 Since the publication of the volume by H.M. Wingler, *Der Bauhaus 1919-1933*, Verlag Gebr. Rasch & Co., Bramsche 1962; 2nd ed., 1968 (Eng. trans. of the 2nd ed., *The Bauhaus*, translated by W. Aabs and B. Gilbert, MIT Press, Cambridge, Mass., 1969) containing a great deal (if not all) the unpublished documentation, the revision of the historical significance of the Bauhaus has continually occupied scholars of modern architecture. Among the most recent contributions may be cited: W. Scheidig, *Le Bauhaus de Weimar*, Bernard Laville, Leipzig 1966; the whole issue of *Controspazio*, 1971, nos. 4/5; *Bauhaus 1919-1929*, catalogue of the exhibition held at the Musée National d'Art Moderne, Paris 1969; and, principally, F. Dal Co, "Hannes Meyer e la 'venerabile scuola' di Dessau," introduction to the Italian edition of the collected writings of H. Meyer, entitled *Architettura o rivoluzione*, Marsilio, Padua 1969. In addition, see the fundamental work by M. Franciscono, *Walter Gropius and the Creation of the Bauhaus in Weimar. The Ideals and Artistic Theories of its Founding Years*, University of Illinois Press, Urbana 1971.

16 Walther Ruttmann, "Berlin: die Symphonie der Grossstadt,"
1927. Film Stills Archive, Museum of Modern Art, New York.

mation of Le Corbusier's *Plan Voisin* (1925) and the transformation of the Bauhaus (1923), contained this contradiction: starting from the particular sector of building production, architecture discovered that the preestablished objectives could be reached only by relating that sector to the reorganization of the city. Thus, just as the necessities singled out by the avant-garde had referred to the sectors of visual communication most directly related to the economic process—architecture and industrial design—so the planning enunciated by architectural and urban theories referred to something other than itself. In this case the something other was a restructuring of production and consumption in general; in other words, the planned coordination of production. In this sense architecture—beginning with itself—mediated realism and utopia. The utopia consisted in obstinately hiding the fact that the ideology of planning could be realized in building production only by indicating that it is beyond it that the true plan can take form; rather, that once come within the sphere of the reorganization of production in general, architecture and urbanism would have to be the objects and not the subjects of the Plan.

Architecture between 1920 and 1930 was not ready to accept such consequences. What was clear was its "political" role. Architecture (read: programing and planned reorganization of building production and of the city as a productive organism) rather than revolution. Le Corbusier clearly enunciated this alternative.

In the meantime, and beginning with just the most politically committed circles—from the *November-*

gruppe to the magazines *MA* and *Vešč* and the Berlin *Ring*—architectural ideology was defined technically. Accepting with lucid objectivity all the conclusions on the "death of the aura" and on the purely "technical" function of the intellectual apocalyptically announced by the avant-garde movements, the central European *Neue Sachlichkeit* adapted the method of designing to the idealized structure of the assembly line. The forms and methods of industrial work became part of the organization of the design and were reflected even in the ways proposed for the consumption of the object.

From the standarized element, to the cell, the single block, the housing project and finally the city: architecture between the two wars imposed this assembly line with an exceptional clarity and coherence. Each "piece" on the line, being completely resolved in itself, tended to disappear or, better, to formally dissolve in the assemblage.

The result of all this was that the aesthetic experience itself was revolutionized. Now it was no longer objects that were offered to judgment, but a process to be lived and used as such. The user, summoned to complete Mies van der Rohe's or Gropius' "open" spaces, was the central element of this process. Since the new forms were no longer meant to be absolute values but instead proposals for the organization of collective life—the integrated architecture of Gropius—architecture summoned the public to participate in its work of design. Thus through architecture the ideology of the public took a great step forward. Morris's romantic socialist dream of an art of all for all took ideological form

17 *Top left*, Vlastislav Hofman, study for an apartment house, 1914.
Top right, Pavel Janak, study for a facade, 1913–1914. *Bottom*,
Vlastislav Hofman, architectural study, 1913.

within the iron-clad laws of profit. Even in this, the ultimate test of the theoretical hypotheses was the confrontation with the city.

5 "Radical" Architecture and the City

In his *Grossstadtarchitektur*, published in 1927, Ludwig Hilberseimer wrote:

The architecture of the large city depends essentially on the solution given to two factors: the elementary cell and the urban organism as a whole. The single room as the constituent element of the habitation will determine the aspect of the habitation, and since the habitations in turn form blocks, the room will become a factor of urban configuration, which is architecture's true goal. Reciprocally, the planimetric structure of the city will have a substantial influence on the design of the habitation and the room.[63]

Thus the large city is, properly speaking, a unity. Reading beyond the author's intentions we may interpret his assertions to mean that, in its structure, the entire modern city becomes an enormous "social machine."

Contrary to the road followed by many German theorists between 1920 and 1930, Hilberseimer chose this particular aspect of the urban economy, isolating it in order to analyze it and resolve its components separately. For the lucidity of his exposition and his reduction of the problems to their essentials, what Hilber-

63 L. Hilberseimer, *Grossstadtarchitektur*, Julius Hoffmann Verlag, Stuttgart 1927. See L. Grassi, introduction to L. Hilberseimer, *Un'idea di piano*, Marsilio, Padua 1967 (Italian ed. of *Entfaltung einer Planungsidee*, Ullstein Bauwelt Fundamente, Berlin 1963).

seimer wrote on the relation between the cell and the urban organism is exemplary. The cell is not only the prime element of the continuous production line that concludes with the city, but it is also the element that conditions the dynamics of the aggregations of building structures. Its standard quality permits its analysis and its solution in the abstract. The building cell understood in this sense represents the basic structure of a production program, from which is excluded any other standard component. The single building is no longer an "object." It is only the place in which the elementary assemblage of single cells assumes physical form. Since these cells are elements reproducible *ad infinitum*, they conceptually embody the prime structures of a production line that excludes the old concepts of "place" or "space." Hilberseimer coherently posed as the second term of his theorem the entire urban organism. The conformation of the cells predisposes the coordinates of the planning of the whole city. The structure of the city, by dictating the laws of assemblage, will be able to influence the standard form of the cell.[64]

In the rigid process of planned production, architecture loses its specific dimension, at least in the traditional sense. Since it is "exceptional" in respect to the homogeneity of the city, the architectural object is completely dissolved. In Hilberseimer's words:

64 From this comes the scheme of the "vertical city", which according to Grassi (*op. cit.*, p. 10) is a theoretical alternative of the "city of three million inhabitants" presented by Le Corbusier in 1922 at the Salon d'Automne. It should also be noted that Hilberseimer—despite his strict detachment, and indeed that of all the "radical" intellectual groups that followed—after his immigration to the United States and a period of self-criticism, did not remain impervious to the myths of the community and nature that were to be among the ideological ingredients of the New Deal.

[Having] to mold large masses according to a general rule dominated by multiplicity, the general case and the law are emphasized and made evident, while the exception is put aside, the nuance cancelled. What reigns is measure, which constrains chaos to be form: logical, univocal, mathematical form.[65]

And again:

The necessity of molding a heterogeneous and often gigantic mass of material according to a formal law equally valid for each element involves a reduction of architectonic form to its most modest, necessary, and general requirement: a reduction, that is, to cubic geometric forms, which represent the fundamental elements of any architecture.[66]

This was not a simple purist "manifesto." Hilberseimer's considerations regarding the architecture of the metropolis—wholly in line with the analogous observations made by Behrens in 1914[67]—constituted a logical deduction made from hypotheses always strictly controlled in their conceptual elaboration. Hilberseimer did not offer "models" for designing, but rather established, at the most abstract and therefore most general level possible, the coordinates and dimensions of the design itself. In this way Hilberseimer—far more than Gropius, Mies, or Bruno Taut, in the same years —made clear what the new tasks were to which architects were called in this phase marked by the reorganization of production.

It is true that Hilberseimer's "city-machine," the im-

65 L. Hilberseimer, *Grossstadtarchitekture, cit.*
66 *Ibid.*
67 See P. Behrens, "Einfluss von Zeit und Raumausnutzung auf Moderne Formentwicklung," in *Der Verkehr*, Jahrbuch des Deutschen Werkbundes 1914, Eugen Diederich Verlag, Jena 1914, pp. 7-10.

age of Simmel's metropolis, seized upon only certain aspects of the new function assigned to large cities by capitalist reorganization. But the fact remains that, in face of the new techniques of production and the expansion and rationalization of the market, the architect as producer of objects had indeed become an inadequate figure. It was now no longer a question of giving form to single elements of the city, nor even to simple prototypes. The real unity of the production cycle having been identified in the city, the only suitable role for the architect was as organizer of that cycle. Carrying the proposition to the extreme, the activity of deviser of models of organization, on which Hilberseimer insisted, was the only one completely reflecting both the necessity of Taylorizing building production and the new role of technician that had become so much a part of this necessity.

With this outlook Hilberseimer could avoid involving himself in the "crisis of the object," noted with disquiet by architects such as Loos or Taut. For Hilberseimer, the "object" did not enter into crisis: it had already disappeared from the panorama of his considerations, and the only situation there demanding his attention was that dictated by the laws of organization. The real value of Hilberseimer's contribution has been seen, correctly, to lie precisely in this.

What, instead, has not been grasped is Hilberseimer's complete rejection of architecture as an instrument of knowledge, as a means of creative research. On this subject even Mies van der Rohe was divided. In the houses on Afrikanische Strasse in Berlin Mies came close to Hilberseimer's position. In the experimental

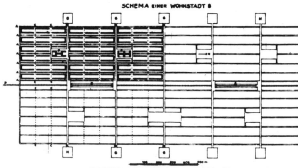

18 Ludwig Hilberseimer, illustrations from *Grossstadtarchitektur*, Stuttgart 1927.

quarter of Weissenhof in Stuttgart he was uncertain. But in the project for a curvilinear skyscraper in glass and iron, the monument to Karl Liebknecht and Rosa Luxemburg, the design for a housing project of 1935, and basically also in the Tugendhat house, he explored the margins of creative exploration still allowed the architect.

We are not here interested in following in detail the developments of this controversy, which runs through the whole history of the modern movement. It should, however, be emphasized that many of the contradictions and obstacles the modern movement encountered stemmed from the attempt to separate technical propositions from creative aims.

Frankfurt planned by Ernst May, Berlin administered by Martin Wagner, the Hamburg of Fritz Schumacher, and the Amsterdam of Cor van Eesteren are the most important chapters in the history of the social-democratic administration of the city. But next to the oases of order of the *Siedlungen*, the experimental quarters or settlements—actually *built utopias* at the edge of an urban reality very little conditioned by them—the historic centers and the productive areas of the city continued to accumulate and multiply their contradictions. And these were in large part contradictions that soon became more decisive than the means architecture had devised to control them.

It was the architecture of Expressionism that absorbed the ambiguous vitality of those contradictions. The *Höfe* in Vienna and the public buildings of Poelzig or Mendelsohn were certainly extraneous to the new methods of urban intervention of the avant-garde movements. They indeed rejected the new horizons discovered by an art that had accepted its own "technical reproducibility" as a means of influencing human behavior. Nevertheless, they seem to assume a critical value, and precisely in regard to the development of the modern industrial city.

Works such as Poelzig's Grosses Schauspielhaus in Berlin, the Chile house and other works in Hamburg by Fritz Höger, and the buildings in Berlin by Hans Hertlin and Ernst and Günther Paulus certainly did not construct a new urban reality. But, resorting to formal exasperations rife with pathos, they commented the contradictions of the operative reality.

The two poles represented by Expressionism and the *Neue Sachlichkeit* again symbolize the inherent division in European artistic culture.

Between, on the one hand, the destruction of the *object* and its substitution by a process to be lived as such, effected by the artistic revolution of the Bauhaus and the Constructivist currents, and, on the other, the exasperation of the *object*, typical of Expressionism's ambiguous eclecticism, there could be no give and take.

But we should not be misled by the merely obvious. This was a controversy between, on the one hand, intellectuals who reduced their own ideological potential to the instrumentation of advanced programs for a production system in the course of reorganization, and, on the other hand, intellectuals who worked by taking advantage of the backwardness of European capitalism. Seen in this light the subjectivity of Häring or Mendelsohn assumes a critical significance in respect to the Taylorism of Hilberseimer or Gropius. Objectively,

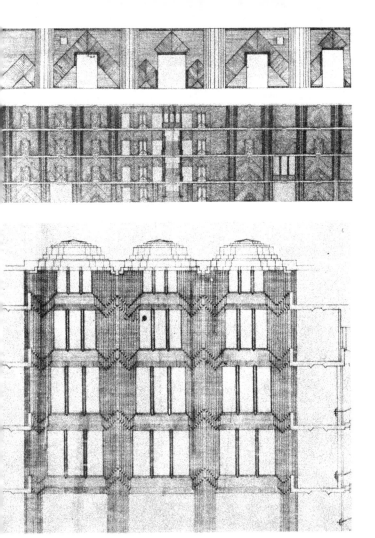

19 Peter Behrens, elevation for the central hall of the Hoechst administrative offices in Frankfurt a. M., 1920–1928.

however, this was a criticism made from a rear-guard position and thus incapable of imposing universal alternatives.[68]

Mendelsohn's self-proclaiming architecture is a creation of persuasive "monuments" in the service of commercial capital. Häring's intimacy of expression plays on the late romantic tendencies of the German middle class. And yet, to present the course of architecture of the twentieth century as a single, unitary cycle is not completely wrong.

The rejection of contradiction as the premise for objectivity and the rationalization of programing proved to be but a partial measure, exactly in the moment of its maximum rapport with the political authorities. The experience of the social-democratic architects of central Europe was based on the unification of administrative power and intellectual proposals. It was thus that May, Wagner, or Taut had political appointments in the administration of social-democratic cities.

68 For this reason I consider very questionable Zevi's recently restated interpretation of Mendelsohn as "an expressionist" and figure of protest. See B. Zevi, *Erich Mendelsohn, opera completa. Architettura e immagini architettoniche*, Etas Kompass, Milan 1970. All Mendelsohn's early work was produced under a Nietzchean acceptance of reality. It would not be difficult to demonstrate that his *collages* on an urban scale (the renovation of the *Berliner Tageblatt* building in Berlin, or the Epstein warehouses at Duisburg), as well as his urban undertakings in Berlin, were thoroughly imbued with the views of German sociology of the early twentieth century concerning metropolitan behavior. Mendelsohn's specific formal means—interpreted correctly by Zevi—were clearly aimed at that *intensification of sensory stimulation (Nervenleben)* that Georg Simmel in his work, mentioned above, recognized as the typical effect of the metropolis on the "metropolitan individual." And it should not be forgotten that for Simmel as for Mendelsohn this intensification of stimuli was only a premise for the achievement of a superior rationality (*Verstand*). Interesting for certain aspects of Mendelsohn are two works usually forgotten by historians of German architecture: K. Weidle, *Goethehaus und Einsteinturm*, Wissenschaftlichen Verlag Dr. Zaugg u. Co., Stuttgart 1929; and W. Hegemann, ' "Mendelsohn und Hoetger ist "nicht" fast Ganz Dasselbe'? Eine Betrachtung Neudeutscher Baugesinnung," *Wasmuths Monatshefte für Baukunst*, XII, 1928, 9, pp. 419-426.

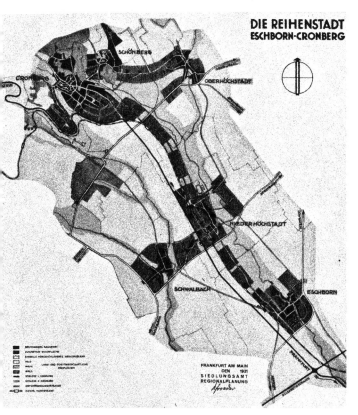

20 Regional plan for the Eschborn-Cronberg system, 1931.

If now it was the entire city that assumed the structure of an industrial machine, solutions had to be found within it for different categories of problems. First of all, that stemming from the conflict between the necessity of globally organizing the machine-city and the parasitic mechanisms of real-estate investment that block the expansion and modernization of the building market and impede the revolution within its technology.

The architectural proposal, the urban model on which it was developed, and the economic and technological premises on which it was based (public ownership of the city soil and industrialized building enterprises conforming to programed urban-production cycles), were all indissolubly connected. Architectural science was totally integrated with the ideology of the plan, and even the formal choices were only variables dependent on it.

All May's work at Frankfurt can be interpreted as the maximum expression of such a concrete "politicization" of architecture. The industrialization of the building yard involved the establishment of a minimal unit of production. The minimal unit fixed upon was the housing project, the *Siedlung*. Within this complex the primary element of the industrial cycle was pivoted on the service nucleus (the *Frankfurter Küche*). The dimensions given the new quarters and their position in the city were decided by the municipal policy on terrain directly administered by the municipality. But the formal model of the new quarter was an open question and thus became the element that gave it its cultural stamp and made "real" the political objectives assumed in full by the architect.

Nazi propaganda was to speak of the Frankfurt settlements as *constructed socialism*. We must see them as realized social democracy. But it must be noted that coincidence of political and intellectual authority served only as pure mediation between structures and suprastructures. This was clear in the organization of the city itself. The closed economy of the settlements reflected the fragmentary character of the undertakings that left intact the contradictions of the city, which was not controlled and restructured as a system in relation to the new decentralized position of the productive centers.

The utopianism of central European architecture between 1920 and 1930 consisted in a relationship of trust established between left-wing intellectuals, the advanced sectors of "democratic capitalism" (think, for instance, of a figure such as Rathenau), and the democratic administrations. Within the working situation the solution to individual problems tended to be presented as highly generalized models (policies of eminent domain and expropriation, technological experimentation, formal elaboration of the housing project as a standard architectural type), but they revealed their limited efficiency when tested in actual fact.[69]

69 A complete study of the social-democratic administration of European cities between the two wars is still lacking. To approach the subject it is necessary to refer to the sources: the issues of the journals *Das neue Frankfurt, Die neue Stadt, Die Form*, etc. (See the volume *Die Form. Stimme des deutschen Werkbundes*, Bertelsmann Fachverlag, Berlin 1969). See in addition: J. Bueckschmitt, *Ernst May*, A. Koch Verlag, Stuttgart 1963; B. M. Lane, *Architecture and Politics in Germany, 1918-1945*, Harvard University Press, Cambridge, Mass., 1968; E. Collotti, "Il Bauhaus nell'esperienza politico-sociale

May's Frankfurt, like the Berlin of Mächler and Wagner, indeed tended to reproduce the models at a social level; to make the city assume the aspect of a productive machine; and to achieve the appearance of a general proletarianization in the urban structure and in the mechanism of distribution and consumption. (The interclass character sought by central European urbanism was an objective continually proposed by the theorists.) But the unity of the urban image—a formal metaphor of the proposed "new synthesis," a sign of the collective dominion over nature and the means of production confined within a new "human" utopia —was not achieved by the German and Dutch architects. Working within the precise policies of a plan for the urban and regional area, they elaborated models of overall applicability. The model of the *Siedlung* is proof of this. But the constant pursuit of this theoretical aim reproduced in the city the disintegrated form of the paleotechnical assembly line. The city remained an aggregate of parts only minimally unified in its functioning. And even within the single "piece"—the workmen's settlement—the unification of methods was quickly revealed to be a means to uncertain ends.

In the specific field of architecture the crisis exploded in 1930 in the Berlin Siemensstadt. It is incredible that contemporary historical study has not yet recognized

della Repubblica di Weimar," *Controspazio*, 1970, no. 4/5, pp. 8-15; *L'abitazione razionale. Atti dei Congressi CIAM, 1929-1930*, edited by C. Aymonino, Marsilio, Padua 1971; M. Tafuri, "Sozialdemokratie und Stadt in der Weimarer Republik (1923-1933)," *Werk*, 1974, no. 3, pp. 308-319. *idem*, "Austromarxismo e città: 'Das rote Wein'," *Contropiano*, 1971, no. 2, pp. 259-311. On the outcome of the German experience see the essay by M. De Michelis, "L'organizzazione della città industriale nel Primo Piano Quinquennale," in the volume by various authors, *Socialismo, città, architettura, cit.*

this famous settlement, planned by Scharoun, as the work in which one of the most serious ruptures within the "modern movement" became evident.

The postulate of a uniform method of design applied in different dimensional scales reveals the utopian character of the Siemensstadt. On a basic urban design (that has been referred, perhaps rightly, to Klee's ironic deformations), Bartning, Gropius, Scharoun, Häring, and Forbat demonstrated that the dissolution of the architectural object in the overall process only emphasized the internal contradictions of the modern movement. Gropius and Bartning remained faithful to the concept of the housing project as an *assembly line*, but contrasting with this were Scharoun's allusive irony and Häring's emphatic organic expression. If the ideology of the *Siedlung* consummated, to use Benjamin's phrase, the destruction of the "aura" traditionally connected with the "piece" of architecture, Scharoun's and Häring's "objects" tended instead to recover an "aura," even if it was one conditioned by new production methods and new formal structures.

The case of the Siemensstadt is, moreover, only the most striking of its kind. Indeed, if Cor van Eesteren's Amsterdam be excepted, between 1930 and 1940 the ideal of the European Constructivist movements, the ideal that had given life to a city of one unified tendency, was decidedly in crisis.

But the crisis lay above all in the twofold failure of the urban policy set in motion by European democratic socialism. As an attempt to control class movements it proved immediately damaging; as an attempt to demonstrate the superiority of building activity directly

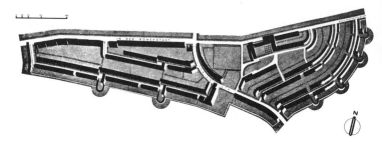

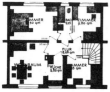

ZWEIFAMILIENWOHNHAUS
ERD- UND OBERGESCHOSS

SIEDLUNG RÖMERSTADT BAUHERR: MIETHEIM A. G.

ZAHL DER WOHNUNGEN									Durchschnittswerte bei den Haupttypen für eine Wohnung				Einrichtungen z. Erleichterung d. Haushaltsführg. und Zentralanlagen
Insgesamt	mit Raumzahl						Zubehör je Wohnung	Wohnfläche qm	Reine Baukosten RM	Gesamtkost. incl. Grundst. u. Aufschließung RM	monatliche Miete-Belastung RM	
	1	2	3	4	5	6						
1211	240							48	Im Bau			
		308						66	Werte stehen daher noch nicht fest			
			226 Einfam Häuser				Küche	75				Frankf. Küche Haus-Zentralheizung u. Warmwasserversorgung
				395 Einfam Häuser			Kammer	88				
					42 Einfam Häuser		Bad	106				
						9		130				

Die Siedlung wurde durch die Mietheim A.-G. in den Jahren 1927/28 auf enteignetem Gelände errichtet. Der Siedlungsplan wurde von Stadtbaurat M a y unter Mitarbeit von Städt. Baurat B o e h m, aufgestellt. Der Entwurf der Wohnungsbauten erfolgte unter Verwendung von wenigen Typen, für die Bauten beiderseits der Straßen an der „Ringmauer" durch den Architekten B.D.A. Schaupp, für die Bauten beiderseits der Straße „Im Heidenfeld" durch den Architekten B.D.A. Blattner, für den Wohnungsblock westlich des Südeinganges der Siedlung an der „Hadrianstraße" durch den Architekten BDA. Franz Schuster, für die übrigen Teile durch Stadtbaurat M a y, Mitarbeiter Architekt B.D.A. C.-H. R u d l o f f.

21 Ernst May and colleagues, Römerstadt settlement, Frankfurt a. M.; plan of the whole, plan of a two-family-type house, and comparative tables, from *Das neue Frankfurt*, 1928, no. 7/8.

managed by the working class and trade union organizations (the Dewog and the Gehag in Germany), the city of the experimental settlements remained extraneous to the processes of a comprehensive reorganization of the productive territory.

There is, however, yet another reason why the balance books of the social-democratic administration of the city closed with a loss. This was precisely the model proposed for the urban undertaking: the housing project, or settlement. The fact is that in themselves these experimental quarters were part of a global antiurban ideology. If this ideology, on the one hand, went back to that of Jefferson, on the other, it was deeply rooted in the tradition of socialist thought. (But not that of Marx: recall the passages on the political significance of the large city in *Capital* and the *Critique of Political Economy*.) At the base of the urban reorganization led by May and Martin Wagner was the postulate of the intrinsic negativeness of the large city. The settlement was thus to be an oasis of order, an example of how it is possible for working-class organizations to propose an alternative model of urban development, a realized utopia. But the settlement itself openly set the model of the "town" against that of the large city. this was Tönnies against Simmel and Weber.[70] In Ernst May's Frankfurt, the renewed technology of the building yards was superimposed on a generally antiurban proposal. Indeed, those new quar-

70 The volume by Ferdinand Tönnies, *Gemeinshaft und Gesellschaft* [Community and Society] appeared in 1887, but his nostalgia for the "original community" as opposed to organized society, expressed an ideology that was to be taken over by radical urbanism between the two wars, as well as by the populist tendencies of the 1950s.

ters testified to the intention of uniting the development of new systems of building production to a frag-
mented and static organization of the city.

But this was not possible. The city of development
does not accept "equilibriums" within it. Thus the
ideology of equilibration also proved a failure.

It should in any case be noted that the antiurban
utopias have their historical continuity reaching back to
the era of the Enlightenment—and here it should not be
forgotten that the first anarchic theories of the necessity
of a "dissolution of cities" appeared in the second half
of the eighteenth century[71]—and embrace the theory of
the Garden City, Soviet decentralization, the regional-
ism of the Regional Planning Association of America,
and Frank Lloyd Wright's Broadacre City. From Jeffersonian anti-industrialism, obviously influenced by
the French physiocratic theories, to Bruno Taut's *Auf-
lösung der Stadt*, which explicitly reflected Kropot-
kin's ideas, to the model of the workmen's settlement (a
heritage of nineteenth-century proposals) and to Broadacre, what is expressed is a strong nostalgia for Tönnies' "organic community," for a religious sect adverse
to external organizations, for a *communion of subjects*
who do not know the anguish of metropolitan alienation.

Antiurban ideology is always presented in anticapi-
talist guise, whether it is a matter of Taut's anarchism,

71 Extremely interesting in this regard is the volume by William Godwin, *En-
quiry Concerning Political Justice*, London 1793, in which Enlightenment
rationalism is pushed to the point of conceiving a society in which the state is
dissolved and the individuals—guided by a self-liberating reason—gather into
small communities without laws or stable institutions. See G. D. H. Cole,
Socialist Thought: the Forerunners (1789-1850), Macmillan, London 1925.

22 Cover of *Das neue Frankfurt*, 1929, no. 7/8, which issue was
given over to a discussion of the problems of traffic.

the socialist ethic of the Soviet urbanists of decentralization, or Wright's domestic rural romanticism.[72] But
this anguished revolt against the "inhuman metropolis" dominated by the money economy is only nostalgia, the rejection of the highest levels of capitalist
organization, the desire to regress to the infancy of
humanity. And when this antiurban ideology is part of
an advanced plan for the reorganization of residential
quarters and regional restructuration—as in the case of
the Regional Planning Association of America[73]—it is
inevitably destined to be reabsorbed and deformed by
the contingent needs of an opposing set of circum-
stances. Indeed, the territorial policy set in motion by
the New Deal was not to satisfy the expectations of
Henry Wright, Clarence Stein, and Lewis Mumford.

The model of the "town" conceived in the rural
terms of the region—taken up again in Italy after 1945
with explicit populist intonations—does not stand up in
face of the new urban dimension created by new levels
of productive organization. The aspiration to the *Gemeinshaft*, to the organic community, significantly very

72 On Wright's ideology of the "wilderness" and the anti-city, see E. Kauf-
mann, Jr., "Frank Lloyd Wright: the 11th Decade," *Architectural Forum*,
CXXX, 1969, no. 5; N. K. Smith, *F. L. Wright. A Study in Architectural Con-
tent*, Prentice Hall, Inc., Englewood Cliffs, N.J., 1966; R. Banham, "The
Wilderness Years of Frank Lloyd Wright," *Journal of the Royal Institute of
British Architects*, December 1969; and principally, G. Ciucci, "Frank Lloyd
Wright, 1908-1938, dalla crisi al mito," *Angelus Novus*, 1971, no. 21, pp. 85-
117, and *idem*, "La citta nell'ideologia e Frank Lloyd Wright. Origini e sviluppo
di Broadacre," in the volume by various authors, *La citta americana dalla
Guerre Civile al New Deal, cit.*, pp. 313-413.
73 On the activity of the Regional Planning Association of America see: R.
Lubove, *Community Planning in the 1920's: the contribution of the RPAA*,
University of Pittsburgh, Pittsburgh, 1963; M. Scott, *American City Planning
since 1890*, University of California Press, Berkeley and Los Angeles 1969; and
F. Dal Co, "Dai parchi alla regione. L'ideologia progressista e la riforma della
città," in the volume by various authors, *La città americana dalla Guerra Civile
al New Deal, cit.*, pp. 149-314.

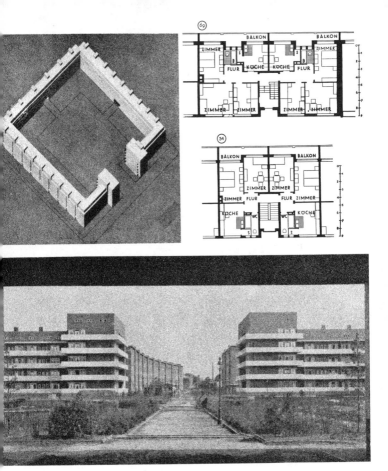

23 Karl Schneider, the residential block "Raum" on the Jarrestrasse in Hamburg, 1929. *Top*, isometric of the complex, and plan of the building types; *bottom*, the complex as built.

strong in the thought of the German left of the 1920s, was destined as a bankrupt hypothesis to succumb to the *Gesellshaft*, to the impersonal, alienated relationship of a society organized in and by the great metropolis.

Extending its manner of existence to the entire region, the metropolis gave rise to the spiralling problem of development-disequilibrium. And indeed the planning theories based on the hypothesis of a reestablishment of equilibrium—and first among them, those of the Soviet Union—were destined to be revolutionized after the great crisis of 1929.

Improbability, multifunctionality, multiplicity, and lack of organic structure—in short, all the contradictory aspects assumed by the modern metropolis—are thus seen to have remained outside the attempts at a rationalization pursued by central European architecture.

6 The Crisis of Utopia:
Le Corbusier at Algiers

Absorb that multiplicity, reconcile the improbable through the certainty of the plan, offset organic and disorganic qualities by accentuating their interrelationship, demonstrate that the maximum level of programing of productivity coincides with the maximum level of the productivity of the spirit: these are the objectives delineated by Le Corbusier with a lucidity that has no comparison in progressive European culture.

In setting out these objectives Le Corbusier is conscious of the threefold front on which architecture must combat. If architecture is now synonymous with the organization of production, it is also true that, beyond production itself, distribution and consumption are the determining factors of the cycle. The architect is an organizer, not a designer of objects. This assertion of Le Corbusier's is not a slogan but an obligatory directive that connects intellectual initiative and the *civilisation machiniste.* As a member of the vanguard of that civilization, in pointing the way and determining its plans (even if only in a partial area) the architect must proceed in several different ways. What he offers directly is the *appel aux industriels* and the building types. The search for an authority capable of mediating the planning of building production and urbanism with programs of civil reorganization is pursued on the political level with the institution of the CIAM. The maximum articulation of form is the means of rendering the public an active and participant consumer of the architectural product.

More precisely, form assumes the task of rendering authentic and natural the unnatural universe of technological precision. And since that universe tends to subjugate nature totally in a continual process of transformation, for Le Corbusier it is the whole anthropogeographic landscape that becomes the subject on which the reorganization of the cycle of building production must insist.[74]

But Le Corbusier discovered also that prudence on the part of the financiers, private interests of the contractors, and the persistence of archaic mechanisms of financial investment—such as that of real estate—dangerously obstruct the development and the "human" yield of that expansion.

Between 1919 and 1929 Le Corbusier studied and established protoypes such as the cell of the Domino house, the Immeuble-Villa, the city of three million inhabitants, and the Plan Voisin for Paris. This patient research made clear and specific the scale and means of

---

74 Le Corbusier's painting should also be analyzed in relation to the active adaptation of the individual to technological reality and the new spatial conditions that such reality imposes. Even after the exhibition at Palazzo Strozzi in Florence (1963) this problem has remained the object of research. In addition to the old article by Nava, not lacking in insight (see A. Nava, "Poetica di Le Corbusier," *Critica d'arte*, III, 1938, pp. 33-38), it has been treated in a few essays of genuine interest: C. Rowe and R. Slutzky, *Transparenz. Le Corbusier—Studien I*, Birkhäuser Verlag, Basel-Eidgenössiche Technische Hochschule, Zurich 1968; C. Green, "Léger, Purism and the Paris Machines," *Art News*, LXVIII, 1970, no. 8, pp. 54-56 and 67; S.A. Kurtz, "Public Planning, Private Planning," *Art News*, LXXI, 1972, no. 2, pp. 37-41 and 73-74.

various types of interventions. In partial realizations that served as laboratory tests, he experimented with general hypotheses and went beyond the models of German "rationalism," intuiting the correct dimension in which the urban problem must be considered.

From 1929 to 1931, with the plans for Montevideo, Buenos Aires, San Paulo, Rio, and finally with the Obus plan for Algiers, Le Corbusier formulated the most elevated theoretical hypothesis of modern urbanism. It is, in fact, still unsurpassed from the point of view of both ideology and form.[75]

In contrast to Taut, May, or Gropius, Le Corbusier breaks up the continuous sequence of architecture-quarter-city. The urban structure, inasmuch as it is a physical and functional unity, is the repository of a new scale of values; it is a statement whose significance is to be sought in its total setting, in the whole landscape.

At Algiers the old Casbah, the hills of Fort-l'Empereur, and the indentation of the coastline are taken up as material to be reutilized, actual *ready-made objects* on a gigantic scale. The new structure that conditions them, by overturning their original significance, creates a unity that before did not exist.

But this maximum conditioning must be matched by a maximum of freedom and flexibility. The economic

75 The whole of Le Corbusier's achievement, which I have sketched here in an all too synthetic manner, needs to be studied completely and in detail. Bryan Taylor's study of the Le Corbusier archive in Paris, relative to the design and execution of the complex at Pessac and to Le Corbusier's earlier studies for workmen's housing, constitutes the beginning of a new trend of research, destined to radically revise the judgments on Le Corbusier as urbanist. See B.B. Taylor, *Le Corbusier et Pessac, 1914-1928*, Foundation Le Corbusier—Harvard University, 1972. Notable also in this regard is the essay by P. Turner, "The Beginnings of Le Corbusier's Education," *Art Bulletin*, LIII, 1971, no. 2, pp. 214-224.

premise of the whole operation is therefore clear. The Obus plan does not require merely a new land statute that by overcoming the anarchic paleocapitalist accumulation of terrain makes all the city soil available for a total and organic reorganization, becoming thus an urban system in the proper sense of the term.[76] In this case the complete availability of the terrain is not enough. The fact is that the industrial object does not presuppose any single given location in the space of the city. Serial production here basically implies a radical overcoming of any spatial hierarchy. The technological universe is impervious to the *here* and the *there*. Rather, the natural place for its operations is the entire human environment—a pure topological field, as Cubism, Futurism, and Elementarism well understood. Thus in the reorganization of the city it is the entire three-dimensional space that must become available.

It is obvious that this conception of the city involves the distinction of two scales of intervention, two cycles of production and consumption.

The restructuring of the total urban space and landscape necessitates the rationalization of the overall organization of the city *machine*. On this scale technological structures and systems of communication must be such that they can construct a unitary *image*. They must so operate that the antinaturalism of the artificial

76 Le Corbusier's experience at Algiers needs still further study. See, however, the chapter dedicated to Le Corbusier's city planning in the small volume by G. Piccinato, *L'architettura contemporanea in Francia*, Cappelli, Bologna 1965; S. von Moos, *Le Corbusier. Elemente einer Synthese*, Verlag Huber, Frauenfeld 1968 (French ed. Horizons, Paris 1971); and R. Panella, "Architettura e città intorno al '30. Algeri nei progetti di Le Corbusier," in the volume by various authors, *Per una ricerca di progettazione*, 3. *Il ruolo dell 'abitazione nella formazione e nello sviluppo della città moderna e contemporanea*, Istituto Universitaria di Architettura di Venezia, Venice 1971.

terrains laid out at various levels and the exceptional character of the road network (highways that run up to the last level of the serpentine block destined for working-class housing) acquire a symbolic value. The freedom of the residential blocks of Fort-l'Empereur take on the emblematic values of the Surrealist avant-garde. Indeed the curvilinear buildings—in the same free forms as the interior of Villa Savoye or the ironic assemblages of the Bestegui attic on the Champs Elysées —are enormous objects that mimic an abstract and sublimated "dance of contradictions."[77]

Also on the scale of the urban structure, now finally resolved in an organic whole, what emerges is the positive quality of the contradictions, the reconciliation of the irrational and the rational, the "heroic" composition of violent tensions. By means of the structure of the image, and only by this means, is the reign of necessity fused with that of liberty. The former is explicated by the rigorously controlled calculations of the plan; the latter, by the recovery within it of a higher human consciousness.

Even Le Corbusier used the technique of shock, but the *objets à réaction poétique* are now connected in an organic reciprocity and it is impossible not to experience the dynamic interrelationship of their forms and

77 The drawings in *Poème de l'angle droit* (Verve, Paris 1955) explain the significance Le Corbusier attributed to the intellectual experience of the passage through the labyrinth. As for Klee, to whose graphic taste these drawings come very near, Order is not a totality external to the human activity that creates it. When the search for a synthesis is enriched by the uncertainty of memory, by equivocal tension, even by the existence of paths that lead to other than the final goal, one arrives at that final goal in the fullness of an authentic *experience*. Even for Le Corbusier the absolute of form is the complete realization of a constant victory over the uncertainty of the future, through the assumption of a skeptical viewpoint as the only guarantee of collective salvation.

24 Le Corbusier, Obus plan for Algiers, 1930, perspective view of the
model. From Le Corbusier and P. Jeanneret, *Oeuvre complète
1929–34*, Artemis, Zurich, p. 141.

functions. On any level that it might be read or used, Le Corbusier's Algiers imposes a total involvement upon the public. It should be noted, however, that the participation to which the public is conditioned is a critical, reflective, and intellectual participation. An "unattentive reading" of the urban images would produce an occult impression. And it is not to be excluded that Le Corbusier counted on such a secondary effect as a necessary indirect stimulus.[78]

"Ward off anguish by absorbing its causes." Le Corbusier's proposals are not, however, limited to this. At the level of the minimal unit of production—the single residential cell—the problem to be faced is that of obtaining the maximum flexibility, interchangeableness, and accommodation to rapid consumption. Within the network of the large structures, constructed on *terreins artificiels* laid out one above the other, the insertion of preformed residential elements is allowed the greatest liberty. For the public this is an invitation to become an

78 Among Le Corbusier's many writings in which the intervention of architecture as an instrument of social integration is put into explicit relief, that relative to the Van Nelle factory in Holland is particularly explicit: "The *Van Nelle* tobacco factory in Rotterdam, a creation of the modern age, has removed all the former connotation of despair from that word "proletarian." And this deflection of the egoistic property instinct towards a feeling for collective action leads to a most happy result: the phenomenon of *personal participation* in every stage of the human enterprise. Labor retains its fundamental materiality, but it is enlightened by the spirit. I repeat, everything lies in that phrase: *a proof of love*. It is to this goal, by means of new administrative forms that will purify and amplify it, that we must lead our modern world. Tell us what we are, what we can do to help, why we are working. Give us plans; show us plans; explain those plans to us. *Unite us.* . . . If you show us such plans and explain them to us, then the old dichotomy between "haves" and despairing "have-nots" will disappear. There will be but a single society, united in belief and action. . . . We live in an age of strictest rationalism, and this is a matter of conscience." (Le Corbusier, "Spectacle de la vie moderne," in *La ville radieuse*, Vincent Fréal et C., Paris 1933, Eng. trans., *The Radiant City*, translated by P. Knight, E. Levieux, and D. Coltman, Orion Press, New York, and Faber and Faber, London, 1967, p. 177.)

The Crisis of Utopia: Le Corbusier at Algiers   131

active participant in the designing of the city. In an explanatory sketch, Le Corbusier even foresees the possibility of inserting eccentric and eclectic elements into the network of fixed structures. The liberty allowed the public must be pushed to the point of permitting the public—the proletariat in the case of the serpentine that winds along the seaside, and the upper middle class on the hills of Fort-l'Empereur—to express its own bad taste. Architecture thus becomes a pedagogical act and a means of collective integration.

In respect to industry, however, that liberty assumes a still greater significance. Le Corbusier does not crystallize the minimal unit of production in standard functional elements, as did May in his *Frankfurter Küche*. On the scale of the single object account must be taken of the exigencies of the continual technological revolution, styling, and rapid consumption, dictated by a dynamic capitalism in expansion. The residential cell, theoretically consumable in brief time, can be substituted at any change of individual necessity—at any change of necessity induced by the renewal of models and residential standards dictated by production.[79]

The significance of the plan thus becomes very clear. The subject of urban reorganization is a public solicited

79 On the basis of these considerations one could refute the thesis of Banham, who from a technological point of view criticizes the masters of the modern movement for their unprogressive stand in relation to the problem of building types. "In opting for stabilised types or norms, architects opted for the pauses when the normal processes of technology were interrupted, those processes of change and renovation that, as far as we can see, can only be halted by abandoning technology as we know it today, and bringing both research and mass-production to a stop." (R. Banham, *Theory and Design in the First Machine Age*, Architectural Press, London 1960, p. 329). It is perhaps superfluous to note that all the architectural science fiction that has proliferated from 1960 up to today, emphasizing the value of the technological processes as "image," is sadly far behind Le Corbusier's Obus plan.

and rendered critically participant in the act of creation. In the impetuous and "exalting" process of continual development and transformation, the industrial vanguard, the "authorities," and the users of the city are involved in theoretically similar functions. From the reality of production to the image and the use of the image, the entire urban machine pushes the "social" potential of the *civilisation machiniste* to the extreme of its possibilities.

We must now try to answer the obvious question. Why did Le Corbusier's plan for Algiers, as well as his later plans for European and African cities and even his lesser proposals, remain a dead letter? We have said that those proposals constitute, even today, the most advanced and formally elevated hypotheses of bourgeois culture in the field of architectural design and urbanism. Is this statement not contradicted by the failures experienced by Le Corbusier?

To this question there are many possible answers, all valid and complementary. It should first of all be noted that Le Corbusier worked as an "intellectual" in the strict sense of the term. He was not, like Taut, May, or Wagner, associated with the local or state authorities. His hypotheses were derived from a specific reality (certainly the particular formation of the terrain and the historical stratification of Algiers are exceptions and the form of the plan that takes account of them is not repeatable), but his method can most surely be broadly applied. From the particular to the universal: the exact contrary of the method followed by the intellectuals of the Weimar Republic. It is also significant that Le Corbusier worked at Algiers for more than four years without an official appointment or compensation. He "invented" his commission, made it generally applicable and was disposed to personally pay for his own active and creative role.

This gives his models all the characteristics of laboratory experiments, and it is impossible that a laboratory experiment become directly in itself a reality. But this is not the whole story. The general applicability of his hypotheses clashed with the backward structures it was intended to stimulate. Since the aim was that of a revolutionizing of architecture in accord with the most advanced tasks of an economic and technological reality still incapable of assuming coherent and organic form, it is hardly surprising that the realism of Le Corbusier's hypotheses was regarded as utopian.

On the other hand, the failure of Algiers—and Le Corbusier's "failure" in general—cannot be correctly understood if not related to the phenomenon of the international crisis of modern architecture. In other words, if not related to the ideological crisis of the "New World."[80]

It is interesting to observe how contemporary historical study has tried to explain the crisis of modern architecture, which is considered to have begun in about 1930 and to have been constantly accentuated up to our own day. Almost all the initial blame for this crisis is attributed to the political involutions of European fascism on the one hand and to Stalinism on the other. Systematically ignored, however, is the appearance, just after the great economic crisis of 1929, of decisive new pro-

80 The ideology of the "New World" as an infinite field of liberating potential is common to both El Lissitzky and Hannes Meyer. See Hannes Meyer's significant article, "Die neue Welt," in *Das Werk*, 1926, no. 7.

tagonists: the international reorganization of capital, the affirmation of systems of anticyclical planning, and the realization of the First Soviet Five-Year Plan.

It is significant that almost all the objectives formulated in the economic field by Keynes' *General Theory* can be found as pure ideology in modern architecture. "Free oneself from the fear of the future by fixing the future as the present" (Negri): the basis of Keynesian interventionism is the same as that of modern art. And in a precisely political sense it is also at the base of Le Corbusier's theories of urbanism. Keynes reckons with the "party of catastrophy" and trys to control its menace by absorbing it at an always new level.[81] Le Corbusier takes account of the reality of class in the modern city and transposes the conflicts to a higher level, giving life to the most elevated proposal for the integration of the public, involved as operators and active consumers in the urban mechanism of development, now rendered organically "human."

Thus our initial hypothesis is confirmed. Architecture as ideology of the plan is swept away by the *reality of the plan* when, the level of utopia having been superseded, the plan becomes an operative mechanism.

The crisis of modern architecture begins in the very moment in which its natural consignee—large industrial capital—goes beyond the fundamental ideology, putting aside the suprastructures. From that moment on architectural ideology no longer has any purpose. The obstinate insistence on seeing its own hypotheses realized

81 See A. Negri, "La teoria capitalista dello stato nel '29: John M. Keynes," *cit.* See also S. Bologna, G. P. Rawick, M. Gobbini, A. Negri, L. Ferrari Bravo, and G. Gambino, *Operai e Stato. Lotte operaie e riforma dello Stato capitalistico tra rivoluzione d'Ottobre e New Deal*, Feltrinelli, Milan 1972.

becomes either a surpassing of outdated realities or an importunate disturbance.

It is in this light that the involutions and anguished controversies of the modern movement since about 1935 up to today can be understood. The general solicitation of a rationalization of cities and regions remains without response, continuing to act as but an indirect stimulus for realizations that are compatible with the partial objectives set from time to time.

It is at this point that something takes place which, at least at first glance, seems inexplicable. The ideology of form seems to abandon its dedication to a realistic out-look and fall back on the alternative position inherent in the dialectic of bourgeois culture. Without aban-doning the "utopia of design," the processes that had concretely surmounted the level of ideology are sub-verted by the redemption of chaos, the contemplation of that anguish which Constructivism seemed to have done away with forever, and the sublimation of dis-order.

Arrived at an undeniable impasse, architectural ideology renounces its propelling role in regard to the city and structures of production and hides behind a rediscovered disciplinary autonomy, or behind neurotic attitudes of self-destruction.

Incapable of analyzing the real causes of the crisis of design, contemporary criticism concentrates all its attention on the internal problems of design itself. It compiles symptomatic ideological inventions in an attempt to offer a new substance to the alliance between the techniques of visual communication and techno-logical utopia. It might also be noted that this alliance is now postulated in terms of an ambiguous "neohumanism," which in comparison to the *Neue Sachlichkeit* of the 1920s has the grave defect of mystifying its own role as mediator between utopia and development. And it is certainly not without significance that the area insisted on for the revival of this alliance is precisely the image of the city.

Thus the city is considered in terms of a suprastructure. Indeed art is now called upon to give the city a suprastructural guise. Pop art, op art, analysis of the urban "imageability," and the "prospective aesthetic" converge in this objective. The contradictions of the contemporary city are resolved in multivalent images, and by figuratively exalting that formal complexity they are dissimulated. If read with adequate standards of judgment this formal complexity is nothing other than the explosion of the irremediable dissonances that escape the plan of advanced capital. The recovery of the concept of *art* thus serves this new cover-up role. It is true that whereas industrial design takes a lead position in technological production and conditions its quality in view of an increase in consumption, pop art, reutilizing the residues and castoffs of that production, takes its place in the rear guard. But this is the exact reflection of the twofold request now made to the techniques of visual communication. Art which refuses to take its place in the vanguard of the production cycle, actually demonstrates that the process of consumption tends to the infinite. Indeed even the rejects, sublimated into useless or nihilist objects which bear a new *value of use*, enter into the production-consumption cycle, if only through the back door.

25 Metropolis: The spire of the Chrysler Building, New York
(William Van Allen, architect; 1928—1930), seen between the RCA
Tower, left (Cross & Cross; 1930—1931), and one of the towers of the
Waldorf-Astoria, right (Schultze & Weaver; 1930—1931). Photo by
Cervin Robinson.

This art that deliberately places itself in the rear guard is also indicative of the refusal to come to terms with the contradictions of the city and resolve them completely; to transform the city into a totally organized machine without useless squanderings of an archaic character or generalized dysfunction.

In this phase it is necessary to persuade the public that the contradictions, imbalances, and chaos typical of the contemporary city are inevitable. Indeed the public must be convinced that this chaos contains an unexplored richness, unlimited utilizable possibilities, and qualities of the "game" now made into new fetishes for society.

The proposals of the new urban ideology may be summed up as follows: architectural and supertechnological utopianism; rediscovery of the game as a condition for involving the public; prophecies of "aesthetic societies"; and invitations to institute a *championship of the imagination*.[82]

There exists a text that in an exemplary way synthesizes all the solicitations made to artistic activity to assume a new persuasive rather than operative role. It is significant that Pierre Restany's "Livre blanc de l'art total," to which we refer,[83] sets forth explicitly all the ideas that arise from the uneasy awareness of the exhaustion of the objectives pursued up to now. The

82 See, as texts symptomatic of the phenomenon: G. C. Argan, *Relazione introduttivo al convegno sulle "strutture ambientali"*, Rimini, September 1968; L. Quaroni, *La Torre di Babele*, Marsilio, Padua 1967; M. Ragon, *Les visonnaires de l'architecture*, Paris 1965; A. Boatto, *Pop art in USA*, Lerici, Milan 1967; F. Menna, *Profezia di una società estetica*, Lerici, Milan 1968. It goes without saying that the grouping together of these works is completely divorced from any consideration of their individual merit.
83 P. Restany, "Le livre blanc de l'art total; pour une esthétique prospective," in *Domus*, 1968, no. 269, p. 50.

result is that, with different words, these "new" proposals for the redemption of art assume the same connotations as the propositions of the historical avant-garde movements, without the clarity or faith in themselves that the earlier movements well had the right to flaunt. Restany writes:

The metamorphosis of languages is only the reflection of the structural changes of society. Technology, in reducing always more the separation between art (synthesis of the new languages) and nature (the modern, technical, and urban reality), plays the determinant role of a necessary and sufficient catalyst.
Beyond its immense possibilities and the unlimited realms it opens to us, technology bears witness to the flexibility indispensible in a period of transition: it makes it possible for the conscious artist to operate, no longer on the formal effects of communication, but on its very terms, on the human imagination. *Contemporary technology indeed permits the imagination to take over:* freed of any normative shackle, of any problem of realization or production, the creative imagination becomes the same as the planetary conscience. *The prospective aesthetic is the vehicle of man's greatest hope: his collective liberation.* The socialization of art directs the convergence of creative forces and production to an objective of dynamic synthesis: the technological metamorphosis. It is through this restructuring that man and reality find their true modern face, that they become *natural,* all alienation past.[84]

The circle closes. Marcusian mythology is adopted to demonstrate that only by immersion in the present relationships of production is it possible to achieve the vaguely identified "collective liberty." It is enough to "socialize art" and place it at the head of technological

84 Emphasis supplied.

"progress." It matters little if the whole cycle of modern art shows clearly the utopianism of such propositions. Thus it is even possible to take up the most ambiguous slogans of the protest of May '68 in France. *"L'imagination au pouvoir"* sanctions the agreement between protest and preservation, between symbolic metaphor and productive processes, between evasion and *realpolitik*.

And this is not all. Reaffirming art's role as mediator, one can even go as far as to assign to art the naturalistic connotations attributed to it in the period of the Enlightenment. "Avant-garde" criticism thus reveals its objectives. The confusion and the ambiguity it preaches for art—taking over as a tool all the conclusions of semantic analysis—are only sublimated metaphors of the crisis and ambiguity of the structures of contemporary cities. Restany continues:

The critical method must contribute to the general application of the aesthetic: supersedure of the individual "work" and multiple production; fundamental distinction between the two complementary orders of creation and production, systematization of operational research and technical cooperation in all domains of experimentation of a synthesis; psychosensory organization of the notion of the game and the spectacle; organization of the environmental space in view of mass communication; insertion of the individual environment in the collective space of urban well being.[85]

Those wishing to examine and judge works realized in accord with such futurologies and appeals to self-

85 *Ibid.* It is clear that I am using Restany's text only as an example of a mythology very widespread among the neo-avant-garde. On the other hand, many of my assertions can be applied to far more profound "disciplinary" attempts at a redemption through utopia. On art as technological utopia, see G. Pasqualotto, *Avanguardia e technologia, cit.*

liberation have only to choose. They could consider the nomad villages of the American hippy communities (here "liberty" and technology are brought together, the temporary housing making use of Buckminster Fuller structures), or the environment designs presented at the 14th Triennale in Milan, or the erotic exhibitionism of Sottsass, Jr., or yet again the interiors and the negative-designs worked up for the exhibition "Italy: The New Domestic Landscape," organized by The Museum of Modern Art in New York in 1972.[86]

In other words, we are witnessing the proliferation of an underground design of protest. But unlike the films of Warhol and Pascali it is institutionalized, propagated by international organs, and admitted to an elite circle. Through industrial design and the creation of "microenvironments" the explosive contradictions of the metropolitan structures, sublimated and subjected to a cathartic irony, enter into private life. The very clever "games" of Archizoom or the creations of sterilized anguish of Gaetano Pesce propose (despite any verbal declaration to the contrary) a "self-liberation" through the private use of the imagination. It is thus that the still-menacing symbols of an Oldenburg or a Fahlström find their utilization in a peaceful "domestic landscape."

The fact that such games, more or less skillful, are given ample space in design is due to the split existing between the building cycle and those industries producing "objects." And one might ask if in this explosion of images we are not witnessing the prelude to a great

86 See the catalogue of the exhibition *Italy: The New Domestic Landscape. Achievements and Problems of Italian Design*, edited by Emilio Ambasz, The Museum of Modern Art, New York 1972.

change in the control of production, already indicated by the new techniques of automation, and that a technological restructuring of building activity would render inevitable.[87]

It is to be noted, however, that, even in the purely ideological field, the futile appeals to *self-disalienation* launched by "negative" design find a response far more sensitive to the "constrained" situation in configural activity from a painter such as James Rosenquist. In presenting his panel *F 111*, Rosenquist responded during an interview published in *Partisan Review*:

Originally the picture was an idea of fragments of vision being sold, incompleted fragments; there were about fifty-one panels in the picture. With one of them on your wall, you could feel something of a nostalgia, that it was incomplete and therefore romantic. That has to do with the idea of the man now collecting, a person buying a recording of the time or history. He could collect it like a fragment of architecture from a building on Sixth Avenue and Fifty-second Street; the fragment even now or at least in the near future may be just a vacant aluminum panel whereas in an earlier period it might have been a fancy cornice or something seemingly more human.
Years ago when a man watched traffic going up and down Sixth Avenue, the traffic would be horses and there would be a pulsing, muscular motion to the speed on the avenue. Now what he sees may be just a glimmer, a flash of static movement; and that idea of what art may become, like a fragment of this painting which is just an aluminum panel.[88]

"A flash of static movement": Rosenquist's *F 111* is one of the most coherent reductions of the metropolitan

87 This observation was developed in my essay "Design and Technological Utopia," in the catalogue cited in the preceding note, p. 388 ff.
88 G. Swenson, "The F-111: An Interview with James Rosenquist," *Partisan Review*, vol. XXXII, no. 4 (fall 1965), pp. 596-597.

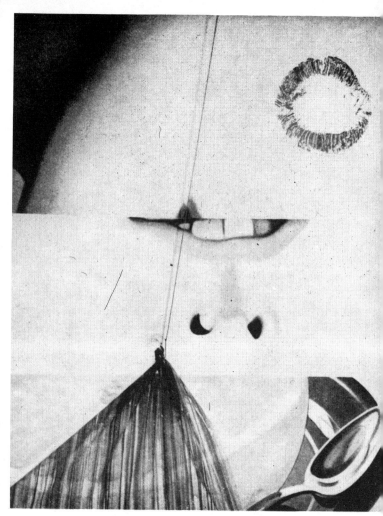

26 James Rosenquist, *Morning Sun*, 1963. According to M. L. Rosenquist, this is the correct orientation of the painting; it was shown upside down in previous editions of this book. M. L. Rosenquist Collection, New York.

experience to the "deadly silence of a sign" produced
by contemporary painting since Mondrian's *Broadway
Boogie-Woogie.* But even Penn Center in Philadelphia,
Kevin Roche's tower in New Haven, or the World
Trade Center by Yamasaki and Roth in Manhattan are
only "fleeting flashes of static emptiness." And not so
much for the deliberate formal emptiness that characterizes them, as for the significance such "fragments"
assume in the contemporary metropolis. Even these
works, according to Rosenquist's metaphor, are fragments that cannot permit themselves to be other than
"a vacant aluminum panel" for disenchanted collectors.[89]

At this point one wonders if there really exists a substantial difference—in the range of our considerations—between such deliberate muteness of form and
the desperate (but sceptical) formal distortions of a
Rudolph or a Lundy (think, in particular, of the Boston
Development Center and Lundy's shoe store on Fifth
Avenue in New York).

In order to "sustain" the metropolitan space, architecture seems obliged to become a spectre of itself. It is
as if it were in this way expiating an original sin, which
is nothing other than its own claim to the right of in-
forming—solely with its own disciplinary means—the
primary structures of the city. Surely it is significant
that in the United States—the country in which this
phenomenon is most evident—it is the university cities
which, in a sort of museum of living architecture, col-

89 Concerning this we may recall the acute interpretation of the World Trade
Center made by Mario Manieri Elia, *L'architettura del dopoguerra in USA, cit.*,
pp. 85-88.

27 Ludwig Mies van der Rohe, Federal Center, Chicago, 1959–1964.
Photo by Hedrich-Blessing.

28 Ludwig Mies van der Rohe, design for the reconstruction of
Battery Park, New York: a photomontage of lower Manhattan with
three residential skyscrapers, 1957–1958. Photo by Hedrich-
Blessing.

lect the formal experiments expelled from Manhattan
or Detroit. What the apodictic products of that *enfant
terrible* of modern architecture, Mies van der Rohe,
prophesied has by now become a reality. In their absolutely asemantic quality the Seagram Building in New
York or the Federal Center in Chicago are objects that
"exist by means of their own death," only in this way
saving themselves from certain failure.[90]

All the same, Mies's "silence" today seems out of
date in comparison to the "noise" of the neo-avant-
garde. But is there really something new in the neo-
avant-garde in respect to the proposals of the historical
avant-garde movements? It would not be difficult to
demonstrate, by means of a scholarly analysis, that, the
renewed ideological interest aside, the margin of novel-

90 There is nothing more erroneous than the interpretation of Mies van der
Rohe in his late works as contradicting the Mies of the 1920s, or the reading of
his late designs as renunciatory incursions into the unruffled realm of the neo-
academic. It is impossible to understand Mies—perhaps the most "difficult" of
the architects of the "golden generation"—if one separates his radical elementarism (which formed part of the tragically ascetic atmosphere of the Berlin
avant-garde of 1919-1922) from the experiences of Dadaism. Indeed, I believe
that his friendship with Kurt Schwitters and Hans Richter and his collaboration
with magazines such as *Frühlicht* and *G* can explain many things otherwise incomprehensible. On the other hand, it should be noted that his relationship
with the *De Stijl* group, on which Zevi insisted (see B. Zevi, *Poetica dell'architettura neoplastica*, Tamburini, Milan 1959), has been denied by Mies himself
in an interview with Peter Blake (see P. Blake, "A Conversation with Mies,"
edited by G. M. Kallmann, in *Four Great Makers of Modern Architecture*, sym-
posium held at Columbia University, Da Capo Press, New York 1970, p. 93
ff.). In order to understand the reason for such an affirmation one must go back
to the completely antiutopian culture of the early Mies, as he expresses it, for
example, in his essay "Rundschau zum neuen Jahrgang," *Die Form*, 1927, no.
2, p. 59. In this sense I reject the interpretation of Mies' late works in the article
by P. Serenyi, "Spinoza, Hegel and Mies: the Meaning of the New National
Gallery in Berlin," *Journal of the Society of Architectural Historians*, XXX,
1971, no. 3, p. 240, or that of S. Moholy-Nagy, "Has 'Less is More' become
'Less is Nothing'?" in *Four Great Makers, cit.*, pp. 118-123. More objective,
even if far from the hypotheses stated here, is the essay by U. Conrads, "Ich
mache ein Bild . . . Ludwig Mies van der Rohe. Baumeister einer strukturellen
Architektur," in *Jahrbuch Preussischer Kulturbesitz 1968*, Grote, Cologne-
Berlin 1969, vol. VI, pp. 57-74.

ty is extremely narrow. In fact—setting aside the Marcusian utopia of a recovery of the future dimension through the Great Refusal accomplished by the imagination—in comparison to the coherence of the historical avant-garde movements there is certainly something less.

How can we, in fact, explain all this insistence on excessive form and the recovery of a specific dimension for art, in light of the necessity of an always greater integration of formal elaboration in the production cycle? It is certainly not without significance that one of the most widely held answers to this query makes reference to studies in the field of semiology and the critical analysis of language. In this way the study of "new foundations" for the language of architecture seeks an objective terrain in order to surmount problems already surmounted.

7 Architecture and Its Double: Semiology and Formalism

It is indeed symptomatic that the subject least explored by current research on the theory of language and systems of communication is that of their historical origins. In other words, what too often remains carefully hidden is the *why* of semiology (and the *why today*). In response to this antecedent and fundamental question it is not sufficient to evoke the inherent difficulties of the various linguistic disciplines as explanation for the current avid interest in the analysis of their own structures.

That an effort is being made to cover the present state of artistic systems of communication with a delicate ideological veil and that the semiological approach serves in this way to nourish futile hopes is beyond question. But it is not enough to merely recognize the existence of this phenomenon we wish to understand.

We might begin by observing that the proliferation of semiological studies relative to various areas of intellectual work (literature, films, architecture, the argument varies little) coincides with the new impulse given to the study of highly formalized languages, such as the *languages of simulation* and *programing languages*.

These researches are made necessary by the new possibilities the extensive use of cybernetics has opened up. Corresponding to the new branches of mathematics created for the study of the dynamic models—the theory of automatons—are new techniques which make it possible to define and analyze artificial-language systems such as the "generalized programing languages," the "conversational languages" used for dialogues between computers, as well as between managers and computers, and the "languages of simulation." Connected as they are to capital's extension of the use of science and automation, these languages are systems of communication that come into being *from a plan of development*. Their function is to articulate, with the maximum efficiency, a project of global planning of the productive universe. In this respect the creation of such "artificial languages" is connected to the development of techniques of scientific prevision of the future and to the use of the "theory of games" in the realm of economic programing. That is to say, we are witnessing the first—still utopian—attempt at capital's complete domination over the universe of development.[91]

Let us now quickly turn our attention to the first systematic studies made in this century on the informational capacity of artistic and nonverbal languages.

The discovery of the fundamental symbolic quality and of the ambiguity of artistic languages, the attempts at "measuring" their "quantum of communication" by means of information theory, and the connecting of their capacity of communication to a departure from

91 See the essays contained in the volume *Linguaggi nella società e nella tecnica* (acts of a congress promoted by Olivetti, Turin, September 14-17, 1968), Milan 1970.

the established code (the *oestraneje*, or semantic distortion, of the Russian formalists),[92] formed the fundamentals of the new techniques of analysis. But they also provoked a series of collateral effects that must be adequately evaluated:

1 In the first place, the "formal" approach to problems of aesthetic communication offered a formidable theoretical basis to the avant-garde movements of the early twentieth century. The influence of the theories of Opojaz on Russian Futurism is only one particularly evident example of this (because in this case the relations between art and the techniques of analysis are very clear and verifiable historically), but the entire theory of the avant-garde can be read in this light.

2 In the second place, it must be born in mind that the contributions of Wittgenstein, Carnap, and Frege established almost simultaneously the areas of pertinence relative to grammar, logic, and semiology. Peirce was thus to be enabled to indicate the conditions of manipulability of the pure sign devoid of any symbolic implication, of any semantic reference.

But had not the *pure sign*, the object devoid of reference to anything but itself, the absolute autonomy of the linguistic "material," been "discovered" already by the avant-garde as early as the years before World War I? In essence Malevich's *Gegenstandlose Welt* was the same as El Lissitzky's *Proun*, the senseless phoneme

92 See V. Erlich, *Russian Formalism*, The Hague 1954, 2nd ed. 1964; G. Della Volpe, "I conti con i formalisti russi," in *Critica dell'ideologia contemporanea*, Editori Riuniti, Rome 1967, pp. 121-137; I. Ambrogio, *Formalismo e avanguardia in Russia*, Editori Riuniti, Rome 1968. On the specific relations between the artistic avant-garde movements and Russian formalism, see my essay, "Il socialismo realizzato e la crisi delle avanguardie," in *Socialismo, città, architettura, cit.*, pp. 43-87.

of the onomatopoeic verses of Hugo Ball or Schwitters, and the collages and photomontages of Hausmann. Van Doesburg's Elementarism or the theses advocated by magazines such as *Mécano*, *G*, or *MA* were only a lucid codification of what the tormented experience of the avant-garde had revealed.

The fact is that the discovery of the possibility of inflecting signs devoid of any significance, of manipulating arbitrary relationships between linguistic "materials" in themselves mute or indifferent, did away with any pretense of art as a "political" expression or protest. The only utopia the art of the avant-garde was able to proffer was the *technological utopia*. This is completely clear in the case of such figures as Moholy-Nagy, Hannes Meyer, Schwitters, or Walter Benjamin. As proof it is sufficient to recall Moholy-Nagy's "Konstruktivismus und das Proletariat," written in 1922.[93] In that essay Constructivist ideology is stripped of all the "revolutionary" aspects attributed to it by the Berlin Dadaists, the *Aktion* group, and the various Soviet

[93] I know this article only from the English translation, "Constructivism and the Proletariat," in the volume edited by R. Kostelanetz, *Moholy-Nagy*, Prager, New York 1970, pp. 185-186. According to Sybil Moholy-Nagy, the original German text was published in the magazine *MA* in the May 1922 issue. In reality this issue of *MA* contains no such article. The unsolved bibliographic question apart, the position taken by Moholy-Nagy in this essay is hardly unique. See, for example, the analogous polemical position taken by Schwitters, who in 1923, together with Arp, Van Doesburg, Spengemann, and Tzara, published a manifesto explicitly directed against the politicization of artistic activity ("Manifest Proletkunst," *Merz*, II, 1923, no. 2). But see also the earlier article by Kurt Schwitters, "MERZ," *Der Ararat*, II, 1921, no. 1, pp. 3-9, as well as the position of Ivan Puni (See H. Berninger and J.-A. Cartier, *Jean Pougny, 1892–1956, 1—Les années d'avant-garde*, Ernst Wasmuth, Tübingen 1972). On these controversies alive in the Berlin circle of the twenties, see the volume by I. B. Lewis, *George Grosz: Art and Politics in the Weimar Republic*, The University of Wisconsin Press, Madison 1971, and my essay "URSS-Berlin, 1922: du populisme à l' 'internationale constructiviste'," in *VH 101*, 1972, no. 7-8, pp. 53-87.

groups. (But this is the same mentality as that of *De Stijl*, as well as of the politically committed groups such as the Czechoslovakian *Devetsjl*.)[94] What is of interest to us here is precisely the "constructive," technical bent inherent in the nihilism of the negative utopia of the avant-garde (from Russian Futurism to Dada).[95] Destroy all the symbolic attributes accumulated by the linguistic signs, purify the signs to the point of annihilation, articulate their interrelationships on the basis of a complete freedom of relations: these are all operations depending directly on the fundamental law of systematic infraction of the rules, the law on which avant-garde theory was structured.

But the elaboration of systems of freely related, manipulable signs and the linking of their means of communication to that sort of *theory of the permanent destruction of sense* inherent in the constant search for an effective ambiguity of the language signifies:

(a) dictation of the conditions according to which the systems of artistic communication can "act" in the everyday world. (And it is in this sense that the semiology of Peirce and Morris is related to the processes summarized here.);

(b) preservation, in spite of all, of a *distance* from

94 On the *Devetsjl* group and on the architectural avant-garde in general in Czechoslovakia, see the article by V. Procházka, "L'attività degli architetti cecoslovacchi in URSS negli anni Trenta," in *Socialismo, città, architettura, cit.*, pp. 289-307.

95 A study might well be made on the whole history of the inevitable and progressive transformation of Futurist and Dadaist mockery into new models of artistic behavior. In fact, in Dada and the best of Marinetti there is implicit in the negation of every value a strong adherence to Weber's *Wertfreiheit*, or in other words to the "freedom from value" already dramatically declared by Nietzsche to be the indispensible condition of action. Nietzsche's song "Yea and Amen" is the goal to which the Dadaist protests inevitably tended, as later the vain "revolutionary" aspirations of Surrealism. On this see the interesting essay by R.S. Short, "La politica del Surrealismo, 1920-1936," *Dialoghi del XX*, 1967, no. 2, p. 29 ff.

29 Carlo Aymonino, central cross section of one of the buildings in the Gallaratese quarter in Milan. The different interior levels, of entrance hall, corridor, etc., are legible on the exterior.

the everyday world, from reality [Max Bense, a theoretician of technological aesthetics, used the term *co-reality (Mitwirklichkeit)* to suitably situate the aesthetic processes in relation to physical reality.];[96]

(c) a setting forth, as the only and authentic "norm" of *work on the word or the language* carried out by avant-garde art, not only a very high degree of uncertainty and improbability—and therefore a high quantum of information—but also a constant alteration of internal relationships. Indeed the avant-garde was dedicated to an *ideology of permanent and programed innovation.*

From what we have stated here it is clear that between modern linguistics and the avant-garde movements there developed—up to at least 1930—a closely knit interrelationship. The complete independence of the sign and its manipulation are at the base not only of semiology and behavioral analysis, but also of the passage of avant-garde art into the realms of production and publicity.

It is hardly by chance that the sector of visual communication most directly connected to the realm of production was the one to be most affected by this passage. Architecture, as an element of the urban phenomenon, fell heir even in this field to the entire heritage of the avant-garde movements. As a premier example, think of Le Corbusier's complex relationship with Cubism and Surrealism.[97] But is was also precisely

96 Concerning this see G. Pasqualotto, *op. cit.*
97 The relations between Le Corbusier and Surrealism have been outlined in the volume by S. von Moos, *Le Corbusier. Elemente einer Synthese*, cit. The subject requires, however, a specific and detailed analysis, which I hope to carry out elsewhere.

in the field of architecture that the greatest contradictions arose in the relations between linguistic analysis and production systems. Once art (architecture) was materially inserted into the mechanisms of the universe of production, its own experimental character, its own character of co-reality, was necessarily compromised.

It is at this point that there occurred a break between linguistics and architecture, proven by the personal and dramatic experience of Mel'nikov. That is to say, by the experience of the most coherent of the Russian architects who tried to translate into an architectural method the formalist theses of Sklovsky or Eichenbaum.[98] In fact, if the communicative system refers only to the laws of its internal structure, if architecture can be interpreted—in its specific aspects—only as linguistic experimentation, and if this experimentation is realized only through an obliqueness, through a radical ambiguity in the organization of its components, and, finally, if the linguistic "material" is indifferent and matters only in the way the various materials react with each other, then the only road to be followed is that of the most radical and politically agnostic formalism. In other words, the formalism most distant—by free and conscious choice—from the very reality that makes it possible for architecture to exist. When Mel'nikov inserted caryatids of an obvious *Kitsch* flavor into designs such as those for the garage on the Seine in Paris or for the Commissariat of Heavy Industry in Moscow, he was

98 On Mel'nikov's architecture, see Y. Gerchuck, "Mel'nikov," *Architektura SSSR*, 1966, no. 8, pp. 51-55 (Eng. trans. in O. A. Shvidkovsky, *Building in the USSR, 1917-1932*, Studio Vista, London 1971, pp. 57-66), and S. F. Starr, "Konstantin Melnikov," *Architectural Design*, XXXIX, 1967, no. 7, pp. 367-373.

respecting in full the laws of semantic distortion and indifference to the linguistic "materials." But at the same time "work on the word" applied to architecture shows all its unproductiveness. (And it is important to note that this is a twofold unproductiveness: on the one hand, in the material sense, inasmuch as strict formalism can respect purely technological laws and programs only with great difficulty; on the other hand, in the political sense, since its necessary extraneousness to reality, its own experimentalism, renders it completely unsuitable for any propagandistic purpose.)

It is in any case a fact that the entire modern movement postulates an internal criticism of its own processes. And it is also well known that the assumption of the task of criticism on the part of art has always corresponded to an annulment of criticism itself.[99]

We see that the historical process outlined in this essay and the question concerning the *why* of the intense present-day repetition of a close relationship between semiology, information theory, and theories of language actually fit together.

The attempt to revitalize architecture by means of an exploration of its internal structures comes about just at the moment when avant-garde studies in the linguistic field are abandoning "ambiguous" communications and taking their place in the heart of the productive un-

99 I tried to elucidate this problem in *Teorie e storia dell'architettura* (3rd ed., Laterza, Rome-Bari 1973, pp. 121-163). I here respond to the criticism of that work advanced by Enrico Tedeschi (E. Tedeschi, "Two Tools of Theory," *Architectural Review*, 1970, March, p. 136), who seems not to have understood my analysis of the historical significance of the linguistic disciplines: no "operative" end can, in fact, be proposed by the criticism of ideologies. This was, instead, understood perfectly by Bruno Zevi, who attacked *Teorie e storia* in his editorial "Miti e rassegnazione storica," *L'Architettura. Cronache e storia*, XIV, 1968, no. 155, pp. 352-353.

30 ASNOVA Group (Bulikin, Budo, Prokorova, Turkus, and the
sculptor Iodko), model for the competition for the Palace of the Soviet
in Moscow, second phase, 1931.

iverse, through the creation of artificial programing languages.

In other words, from analysis of the ideology of innovation to direct intervention in the real processes of innovation. This is the course followed by contemporary linguistics, at least from a perspective that includes capitalist development. This corresponds to an analogous but opposite course followed by avant-garde art. From the utopian model, the aim of which is the prefiguration of a "total" resolution of the technological universe, avant-garde art is reduced to an appendage of that universe in the course of the latter's realization. The experimental character of the neo-avant-garde fools no one as to its real intentions.[100]

Rediscovering—as happened in the 1960s—a possible avant-garde role for architecture, and concurrently turning to the use of the analytical instruments of the science of communication (here it matters little with what superficiality or approximation), has meant opening a gap between some new experiences and the traditional utopia of the modern movement. At the same time, it has also meant returning to those internal contradictions with which Russian formalism had already collided. Thus the insistent and acritical reevaluation of the experiences of the Soviet avant-garde on the part of Western critics is not surprising.

But, on the other hand, to reduce architecture to an "ambiguous object" within that total *Merz*, the con-

---

100 See H. M. Enzensberger, "L'aporia dell'avanguardia," *Angelus Novus*, 1964, no. 2, pp. 97-116, and the essays by F. Fortini, "Due avanguardie," and G. Scalia, "La nuova avanguardia, o della 'miseria della poesia'," in the volume by various authors, *Avanguardia e neoavanguardia*, Sugar, Milan 1964, p. 95 ff. and p. 22 ff.

temporary city, signifies accepting completely the marginal and suprastructural role which the present capitalist use of land assigns to a purely ideological phenomenon like architecture.

We should not be scandalized by that. Rather, what amazes is that architectural self-criticism does not go to the root of the matter and has need to hide behind new ideological schemes borrowed from the semiological approach.

This phenomenon is easily explained. Through semiology architecture seeks its own meaning, while tormented by the sense of having lost its meaning altogether. In this is clearly to be seen a further contradiction. An architecture that has accepted the reduction of its own elements to pure signs, and the construction of its own structure as an ensemble of tautological relationships that refer to themselves in a maximum of "negative entropy"—according to the language of information theory—cannot turn to reconstructing "other" meanings through the use of analytic techniques which have their origins in the application of neo-positivist theories.

Nevertheless, the semantic analysis of the language has stimulated a resurgence of an ideology of the artistic-literary avant-garde. The pretention of the historical avant-garde, and in the 1960s and 70s of the neo-avant-garde, of presenting work as a critical experimentation of the articulation of the language, should thus be measured against the reality of concrete and productive work on the new possibilities of programed communication.

Furthermore, it should be noted that the artistic con-

31 Louis Kahn, model of a design for the Philadelphia College of Art, 1966. From V. Scully, *American Architecture and Urbanism*, Praeger, New York 1969, p. 223.

ception of indeterminateness, of the open-ended work, of ambiguity raised to an institution, is concentrated—in a large part of the cases—precisely in fields defined by the new techniques of man-machine communication. The case of music *ex machina* is only the most explicit example of this.

It is no longer ideology that, after having assumed utopian connotations, suggests new lines of work to the programers. Work on the materials of communication (i.e., all the techniques of visual, literary, or musical communication and their derivatives) no longer serves as an anticipation of the lines of development: the technique of prognostication, by doing away with final models, nullifies the role of the new ideologies.

Here too the process is symptomatic. Excluded from development, ideology turns against development itself. In the form of protest, it attempts a final recovery. No longer enabled to present itself as utopia, ideology indulges in nostalgic contemplation of its own outmoded roles, or disputes with itself. And it is well known from Baudelaire and Rimbaud that for modern art internal disputation is a means of survival.

The fact remains, however, that any possibility of *external* elaboration of intellectual work is precluded. The illusion of *external* work can come only from the revolt against intellectual work itself, expressed by the consecration of its impotence. Beyond this there is the plunge backward, the "courage to speak of roses," the foundering in the "happy era" of bourgeois *Kultur*: ideology as "sublime" uselessness. But it is not by pure chance that historically the fate of formalism is always to end by the *work on form* being used for advertising.

32 Gae Aulenti, house of an art collector, Milan, 1970.

A completely structuralist criticism, however, can never "explain" the sense of a work. It can do no more than "describe" it, since the only logic at its disposal is that based on *yes-no, correct-incorrect*, precisely analogous to the mathematical logic that guides the functioning of an electronic brain. (It is not accidental that Max Bense refers directly to the theses of R. S. Hartmann on the *mathematical measurement of value*.)[101] In the era of the reproducibility of the work of art, the structure of the processes of its formation—even when a calculator does not intervene in its design—is governed by the logic of automation. The pictures Moholy-Nagy made on the telephone, in 1922, were not only prophecies of present-day procedures of programed assemblage in highly industrialized architecture, but also a complete clarification of the conditions of existence of a work of art that does not want to turn out to be—as Adorno would like—regressive utopia, "conscious" nonsense about its own alienation.

Thus there is but one contribution a consistent structuralism can offer to present-day architecture and art: the exact dimension of its own functionality in the universe of capitalist development, in the universe of integration.

This, however, is exactly what architecture does not

101 M. Bense, "Zusammenfassende Grundlegung moderner Aesthetik," in *Aesthetica*, Agis Verlag, Baden-Baden 1965, Part V, p. 319 ff. Concerning this Pasqualotto has written: "It is true that the value of an aesthetic object is not inherent to it. It is, however, also true that the value attributed to it is not a 'value' understood traditionally, according to pure axiological categories or according to parameters of conscience, but it is identified with its *describability*. In other words, the *qualities* of value, being describable quantities, lose any aura of metaphysical indeterminateness and can be circumscribed within the area of measurable quantitative phenomenon. Evaluation thus becomes a simple description." (G. Pasqualotto, *Avanguardia e tecnologia*, cit. p. 30.)

want and cannot accept. It is also what structuralism—in its many different expressions—is not disposed to recognize as its task. The reason for this is that
semiology itself, despite its complex relationship with
the structural method, is today an ideology; more exactly, an ideology of communication.[102] The single and
collective universe of development must be bound
together by a band of communications capable of
repairing any eventual break, of settling every strife,
and of rendering productive contradiction itself. Thus
the *poetry of ambiguity* corresponds perfectly to the
project wherein the public is a protagonist of the urban
universe by which it is managed. Important in this
regard are Bense's observations on the analogy existing
between the structures of abstract expressionist painting (*Farbtexturen*) and the structures of communication
of the metropolitan landscape (*Geschwindigkeitstex-
turen*).[103]

Modern urbanism—inasmuch as it is a utopian
attempt to preserve a form for the city, or, rather, to
preserve a principle of form within the dynamics of urban structures—has not been able to realize its models.
And yet within urban structures the whole contribution of the historical avant-garde lives on with a particular pregnancy. The city as an advertising and self-ad-
vertising structure, as an ensemble of channels of communication, becomes a sort of machine emitting inces-
sant messages: indeterminacy itself is given specific

102 See M. Cacciari, "Vita Cartesii est simplicissima," *Contropiano*, 1970, no.
2, pp. 375-399.
103 See M. Bense, "Urbanismus und Semiothik," in *Einführung in die infor-
mationstheoretische Aesthetik*, Rowohlt Taschenbuch Verlag, Hamburg 1969,
II, p. 136.

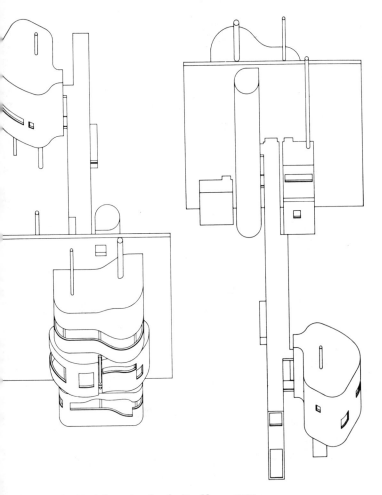

33 John Hejduk, project for the Bye House, 1973.

34 Yamasaki and Roth, World Trade Center, New York, seen against the eighteenth-century steeple of St. Paul's church. Photo by Cervin Robinson.

form, and offered as the only determinateness possible for the city as a whole. In this way form is given to the attempt to make the language of development live, to make it a concrete experience of everyday life.

With this we are back again to our initial subject. It is not sufficient to create *languages of the plan* artificially. It is, however, necessary to immerse the public in the *image of development*, in the city as a programed network of communications, the subject of which is always the "necessity" of the capitalist plan of integration. (In this regard Richard Meier's analyses are explicit.)[104] It is therefore not really permissible to ask if the techniques of linguistic analysis can be utilized in the abstract by historical research. From our point of view we may only examine whether or not it is opportune to use certain parameters of those techniques as a critical means deliberately "external" to the work considered. The conciliatory embrace of Marxism and structuralism excluded, one truth does remain: ideology, despite all its ineffectiveness, has its own structure; and, like all structures it is both historical and transient. To bring its specific characteristics to light, and evaluate its degree of usefulness with respect to the general aims proposed by the dominant forces in any given phase of development, is today the only contribution a criticism that is not purely descriptive can offer.

104 R. L. Meier, *A Communications Theory of Urban Growth*, MIT Press, Cambridge, Mass., 1962.

8 Problems in the Form of a Conclusion

It is certainly not easy, however, to integrate the afore-mentioned useful criticism with a type of designing that deliberately flees confrontation with the most pressing problems of the present situation.

Undeniably, we are here faced with various concomitant phenomena. On the one hand, building production taken as an element of comprehensive planning continues to reduce the usefulness of architectural ideology. On the other hand, economic and social contradictions, which explode in an always more accelerated way within urban agglomerations, seem to halt capitalist reorganization. Faced with the rationalization of the urban order, present-day political-economic forces demonstrate that they are not interested in finding the ways and means to carry out the tasks indicated by the architectural ideologies of the modern movement.

In other words, the ineffectiveness of ideology is clear. Urban approximations and the ideologies of the plan appear as old idols, to be sold off to collectors of antique relics.

Faced with the phenomenon of capital's direct management of land, the "radical" opposition (including portions of the working class) has avoided a confrontation with the highest levels attained by capitalist development. It has instead inherited the ideologies which capital used in the first phases of its development, but has since rejected. In this way it mistakes secondary contradictions for primary and fundamental ones.

The difficulty of the struggle for urban legislation, for the reorganization of building activity, and for urban renewal, has created the illusion that the fight for planning could in itself constitute an objective of the class struggle.

And the problem is not even that of opposing bad plans with good ones. If, however, this were done with the cunning of the lamb, so to speak, it could lead to an understanding of the factors conditioning the structures of the plan that in each case correspond with the contingent objectives of the working class. This means that giving up the dream of a "new world" arising from the realization of the principle of Reason become the Plan involves no "renunciation." The recognition of the uselessness of outworn instruments is only a first necessary step, bearing in mind the ever-present risk of intellectuals taking up missions and ideologies disposed of by capital in the course of their rationalization.[105]

It is clear, however, that any struggle whatsoever on

105 In a seminal essay Mario Tronti has written: "We have before us no longer the great abstract syntheses of bourgeois thought, but the cult of the most vulgar empiricism as the practices of capital; no longer the logical system of knowledge, the scientific principles, but a mass without order of historical facts, disconnected experiences, great deeds that no one ever conceived. Science and ideology are again mixed and contradict one another; not, however, in a systematization of ideas for eternity, but in the daily events of the class struggle. . . . All the functional apparatus of bourgeois ideology has been consigned by capital into the hands of the officially recognized working class movement. Capital no longer manages its own ideology; it has it managed by the working class movement. . . . This is why we say that today the criticism of ideology is a task that concerns the working class point of view and that only in a second instance regards capital" (M. Tronti, "Marx, forza lavoro, classe operaia," in *Operai e capitale*, Einaudi, Torino 1966, p. 171 ff.

the part of the working class over the urban and regional structure must today reckon with programs of great complexity. This is true even when that complexity is due to the contradictions within the economic cycle as a whole, as in the case of the processes presently apparent in the area of building activity. Beyond the criticism of ideology there exists the "partisan" analysis of such a reality, in which it is always necessary to recognize the hidden tendencies, the real objectives of contradictory strategies, and the interests connecting apparently independent economic areas. It seems to me that, for an architectural culture that would accept such a terrain of operations, there exists a task yet to be initiated. This task lies in putting the working class, as organized in its parties and unions, face to face with the highest levels achieved by the dynamics of capitalist development, and relating particular moments to general designs.

But to do that it is necessary to recognize, even in the area of planning techniques, the new phenomena and new participant forces.

I have mentioned earlier the crisis, in the disciplines related to programing, of what we might define as the ideology of equilibrium. It is, on the one hand, the history of the Soviet five-year plans and, on the other, the teachings of post-Keynesian economic theories which sanction this crisis. [106] Even *equilibrium* is seen to be an unfeasible idol when applied to the dynamics of a

106 In regard to the economic history of the USSR in the initial phase of the first five-year plan, see *Contropiano*, 1971, no. 1, dedicated entirely to the problems of industrialization in the Soviet Union; in particular, M. Cacciari, "Le teorie dello sviluppo," p. 3 ff., and F. Dal Co, "Sviluppo e localizzazione industriale," p. 81 ff.

given region. Indeed the present efforts to make equilibriums work, to connect crisis and development, technological revolution and radical changes of the organic composition of capital, are simply impossible. To aim at the pacific equilibration of the city and its territory is not an alternative solution, but merely an anachronism.

The analytic models and the prognostications of the localization of productive centers prepared from the thirties up to today, by Kristaller, Lösch, Tinbergen, Bos, etc., should be judged, not so much for their specific insufficiencies or with ideological criteria, but rather for the economic hypothesis they presuppose. Significant indeed is the ever-growing interest in Preobražensky, a Soviet theorist of the twenties. Increasingly clear is the role Preobražensky played as forerunner of a theory of the plan based explicitly on dynamic development, on organized disequilibrium, on interventions that presuppose a continual revolution of mass production.[107]

It should be observed, however, that programing in individual areas—also for the closed circle that is formed between the technique of intervention and its particular ends—has for the most part up to today operated on the the basis of eminently static models, following a strategy based on the elimination of disequilibriums. The change from the use of static models to the creation of dynamic models seems to be the task posed today by the necessity of capitalist development to update its programing techniques.

107 See M. Cacciari, "Le teorie dello sviluppo," *cit.* A systematic study of the theories of Preobražensky is presently being prepared by M. Cacciari and C. Motta.

Instead of simply reflecting a "moment" of development, the plan now takes on the form of a new political institution.[108]

It is in this way that interdisciplinary exchange pure and simple—a failure even at the practical level—is to be radically surpassed.

Horst Rittel has clearly demonstrated the implica-

108 The appeal recently made by Pasquale Saraceno, to go beyond what he calls programs of objectives to programed action of a general type, falls within that conception of the plan which does away with the schematizations and compartmented theories of planning elaborated between 1950 and 1960. Saraceno writes: "If programing is of a general character it has in substance the goal—completely different [in respect to the vast projects that cover various given sectors of public action]—of composing into a system all the actions undertaken in the public sphere. Programing thus becomes a procedure providing a means of comparing the costs of all the various proposed governmental undertakings, as well as of comparing the total of such costs to the total foreseeable resources. The adoption of a similar procedure would make it more appropriate to speak of a programed society than of a programed economy" (P. Saraceno, *La programmazione negli anni '70*, Etas Kompass, Milan 1970, p. 28). It should be noted that Saraceno's "general program" does not at all constitute a binding plan: its only official duty is "to make known from time to time—probably at intervals not longer than one year—the state of the system" (*op. cit.*, p. 32). Significant is the request for new institutions capable of realizing the coordination. The positive evaluation of the method followed in the formulation of *Progetto 80* (a report on the economic and urban situation in Italy, and on the possibilities of development by 1980, prepared by a team of economists and town planners in 1968–1969 for the Ministry of Development) confirms the line of thinking adopted. Saraceno asks: "What, in fact, is *Progetto 80?* It is a systematic review of the national problems that at *this* moment are judged of greatest importance, as well as of the new institutions which could better than those existing set in motion the means to a solution of these problems. If our public sphere were already ordered in a *system* in the sense defined above, the authors of that document would have produced what has been termed a *program-verification*" (*op. cit.*, p. 52). Despite the fact that even Saraceno's technical prospectives are not without a utopian residue—see his plea for "an ordinance by virtue of which the social forces might morally [*sic*] adhere to the process of utilization of resources required for the solution of the problems" (*op. cit.*, p. 26)—his criticism of the five-year plan of 1966–1970 adheres to an institutional transformation of the control of development, correctly singled out in the note by Sandro Mattiuzzi and Stefania Potenza, "Programmazione e piani territoriali: l'esempio del Mezzogiorno," *Contropiano*, 1969, no. 3. pp. 685-717. That Saraceno's opinions are part of a vast current restructuring of the practice and theory of programming is proven by the whole series of voices raised in favor of the *plan* as a "continually and completely exercised policy." See G. Ruffolo, "Progetto 80: scelte, impegni, strumenti," *Mondo economico*, 1969, no. 1.

tions of the insertion of "decision theory" into self-pro-
graming cybernetic systems. (And it is logical to take
for granted that such a level of rationalization still in
large part represents a utopian model.) Rittel has
written:

Systems of values can no longer be considered established for long periods. What can be wanted depends
on what can be made possible, and what must be made
possible depends on what is wanted. Ends and functions of utility are not independent measures. They
have a relationship of implication in the decisional am-
bit. Representations of value are controllable within
broad limits. Faced with the uncertainty of future alternative developments, it is absurd to wish to construct
rigid decisional models that furnish strategies over long
periods.[109]

Decision theory must assure the flexibility of the
"systems that make decisions." It is clear that the
problem is here no longer purely that of the criteria of
value. The question to which an advanced level of
programing must respond is, "What systems of values
are generally coherent and guarantee the possibility of
adaptation and therefore of survival?"[110]

For Rittel it is thus the very structure of the plan that
generates its systems of evaluation. All opposition
between plan and "value" falls away, precisely as
recognized in Max Bense's lucid theorizing.[111]

109 H. Rittel, *Ueberlegungen zur wissenschaftlichen und politischen
Bedeutung der Entscheidungstheorien*, report of the Studiengruppe für Sys-
temforschung, Heidelberg, p. 29 ff., now available in the volume edited by H.
Krauch, W. Kunz, and H. Rittel, *Forschungsplanung*, Oldenbourg Verlag,
Munich 1966, pp. 110-129.
110 *Ibid.*
111 Pasqualotto has written: "The various steps followed by Bense in his
analysis represent the necessary premise and the very basis of his general conclusions, and at the same time demonstrate the absolute inadequacy of the

The consequences of such phenomena, here barely touched upon, for the structure of planning and for the organization of designing, constitute a still completely open problem. It is, however, a problem which must be faced today and in regard to which didactic experimentation must take a position.

Viewed in this light, what remains of the role played historically by architecture? Up to what point does architecture's immersion in these processes render it a pure economic factor? And to what extent are decisions taken in its own specific sphere reflected in larger systems? The present-day situation in architecture makes it difficult to find coherent answers to these questions.

The fact is that, for architects, the discovery of their decline as active ideologists, the awareness of the enormous technological possibilities available for rationalizing cities and territories, coupled with the daily spectacle of their waste, and the fact that specific design methods become outdated even before it is possible to verify their underlying hypotheses in reality, all create an atmosphere of anxiety. And ominously present on the horizon is the worst of the evils: the decline of the architect's "professional" status and his introduction

policy proposed by Benjamin to the reality of technological integration. The chain of processes which constitute the radical formalization of the elements and structures, of the value and judgments that belong to the area of aesthetics and that of ethics, has proved to be completely functional in revealing the technical intentionality (*technische Bewusstsein*) which represents its foundation. In turn, that technical intentionality presents itself as the determining factor in the construction of a 'new subjectivity', which works for the final goal of a 'new synthesis': the thread of technical intentionality which weaves its way through the technological civilization ends in *integration*. But the realization of this integration evidently does not depend solely on the organic character of an ideology of technology but, rather, in large part on the elaboration of a *policy* of technology" (G. Pasqualotto, *Avanguardia e tecnologia, cit.,* pp. 234-235).

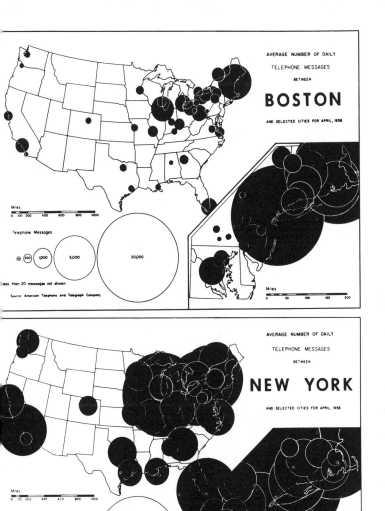

35 Intensity of telephone communications going out from Boston and New York. N. Gustafson diagrams, from *Megalopolis*, Twentieth Century Fund, New York 1961.

into programs where the ideological role of architecture is minimal.

This new professional situation is already a reality in countries of advanced capitalism. The fact that it is feared by architects and warded off with the most neurotic formal and ideological contortions is only an indication of the political backwardness of this group of intellectuals.

Architects, after having ideologically anticipated the iron-clad law of the plan, are now incapable of understanding historically the road travelled; and thus they rebel at the extreme consequences of the processes they helped set in motion. What is worse, they attempt pathetic "ethical" relaunchings of modern architecture, assigning to it political tasks adapted solely to temporarily placating preoccupations as abstract as they are unjustifiable.

Instead, there is a truth that must be recognized. That is, that the entire cycle of modern architecture and of the new systems of visual communication came into being, developed, and entered into crisis as an enormous attempt—the last to be made by the great bourgeois artistic culture—to resolve, on the always more outdated level of ideology, the imbalances, contradictions, and retardations characteristic of the capitalist reorganization of the world market and productive development.

Order and disorder, understood in this way, no longer oppose each other. Seen in the light of their real historical significance there is no contradiction between Constructivism and the "art of protest"; between the rationalization of building production and the subjectivism of abstract expressionism or the irony of pop art;

between capitalist plan and urban chaos; between the ideology of planning and the "poetry of the object."

By this standard, the fate of capitalist society is not at all extraneous to architectural design. The ideology of design is just as essential to the integration of modern capitalism in all the structures and suprastructures of human existence, as is the illusion of being able to oppose that design with instruments of a different type of designing, or of a radical "antidesign."

It is even possible that there exist many specific tasks for architecture. What is of greater interest to us here is to inquire how it is possible that up to now Marxist-inspired culture has, with a care and insistence that it could better employ elsewhere, guiltily denied or covered up a simple truth. This truth is, that just as there cannot exist a class political economy, but only a class criticism of political economy, so too there cannot be founded a class aesthetic, art, or architecture, but only a class criticism of the aesthetic, of art, of architecture, of the city itself.

A coherent Marxist criticism of the ideology of architecture and urbanism could not but demystify the contingent and historical realities, devoid of objectivity and universality, that are hidden behind the unifying terms of art, architecture, and city. It would likewise recognize the new levels attained by capitalist development, with which recognitions the class movements should be confronted.

First among the intellectual illusions to be done away with is that which, by means of the image alone, tries to anticipate the conditions of an architecture "for a liberated society." Who proposes such a slogan avoids

36 Aldo Rossi, *L'architecture assassinée*, hand-painted etching, 1975.
M. Tafuri, Rome.

asking himself if, its obvious utopianism aside, this objective is persuable without a revolution of architectural language, method, and structure which goes far beyond simple subjective will or the simple updating of a syntax.

Modern architecture has marked out its own fate by making itself, within an autonomous political strategy, the bearer of ideals of rationalization by which the working class is affected only in the second instance. The historical inevitability of this phenomenon can be recognized. But having been so, it is no longer possible to hide the ultimate reality which renders uselessly painful the choices of architects desperately attached to disciplinary ideologies.

"Uselessly painful" because it is useless to struggle for escape when completely enclosed and confined without an exit. Indeed, the crisis of modern architecture is not the result of "tiredness" or "dissipation." It is rather a crisis of the ideological function of architecture. The "fall" of modern art is the final testimony of bourgeois ambiguity, torn between "positive" objectives and the pitiless self-exploration of its own objective commercialization. No "salvation" is any longer to be found within it: neither wandering restlessly in labyrinths of images so multivalent they end in muteness, nor enclosed in the stubborn silence of geometry content with its own perfection.

For this reason it is useless to propose purely architectural alternatives. The search for an alternative within the structures that condition the very character of architectural design is indeed an obvious contradiction of terms.

Reflection on architecture, inasmuch as it is a criticism of the concrete "realized" ideology of architecture itself, cannot but go beyond this and arrive at a specifically political dimension.

Only at this point—that is after having done away with any disciplinary ideology—is it permissible to take up the subject of the new roles of the technician, of the organizer of building activity, and of the planner, within the compass of the new forms of capitalist development. And thus also to consider the possible tangencies or inevitable contradictions between such a type of technical-intellectual work and the material conditions of the class struggle.

The systematic criticism of the ideologies accompanying the history of capitalist development is therefore but one chapter of such political action. Today, indeed, the principal task of ideological criticism is to do away with impotent and ineffectual myths, which so often serve as illusions that permit the survival of anachronistic "hopes in design."

List of Illustrations